Risk and Risk Taking
in Health and Social Welfare

of related interest

Surviving Fears in Health and Social Care
The Terrors of Night and the Arrows of Day
Martin Smith
ISBN 1 84310180 7

Managing Sex Offender Risk
Edited by Hazel Kemshall and Gill McIvor
ISBN 1 84310 197 1
Research Highlights in Social Work 46

Risk Assessment in Social Care and Social Work
Edited by Phyllida Parsloe
ISBN 1 85302 689 1
Research Highlights in Social Work 36

Community Care Practice and the Law
Third Edition
Michael Mandelstam
ISBN 1 84310 233 1

Good Practice in Risk Assessment and Risk Management 1
Edited by Hazel Kemshall and Jacki Pritchard
ISBN 1 85302 338 8
Good Practice in Social Work 3

Good Practice in Risk Assessment and Risk Management 2
Protection, Rights and Responsibilities
Edited by Hazel Kemshall and Jacki Pritchard
ISBN 1 85302 441 4
Good Practice in Social Work 5

Good Practice in Working with Violence
Edited by Hazel Kemshall and Jacki Pritchard
ISBN 1 85302 641 7
Good Practice in Social Work 6

Risk and Risk Taking in Health and Social Welfare

Mike Titterton

Jessica Kingsley Publishers
London and Philadelphia

First published in 2005
by Jessica Kingsley Publishers
116 Pentonville Road
London N1 9JB, UK
and
400 Market Street, Suite 400
Philadelphia, PA 19106, USA
www.jkp.com

Copyright © Mike Titterton 2005

Library of Congress Cataloging in Publication Data
Titterton, Mike.
    Risk and risk taking in health and social welfare / Mike Titterton. – 1st American pbk. ed.
    p. cm.
    Includes bibliographical references and index.
    ISBN 1-85302-482-1 (pbk.)
    1. Health risk assessment. 2. Social service. I. Title.
    RA427.3.T56 2005
    362.1--dc22

                                   2004017941

British Library Cataloguing in Publication Data
A CIP catalogue record for this book is available from the British Library

ISBN-13: 978 1 85302 482 5
ISBN-10: 1 85302 482 1

Printed and Bound in Great Britain by
Athenaeum Press, Gateshead, Tyne and Wear

Contents

Acknowledgements

The author would like to thank all those people who have taken part in training courses and those who participated in the research described here. They are too numerous to mention here: they include managers and frontline staff in multidisciplinary settings, as well as service users and informal carers. He would also like to thank those training commissioners with whom the author enjoyed many stimulating discussions about risk and risk taking, particularly Diarmid Murray, formerly of Shetland Social Work Department, and Brian Smith of the Mungo Foundation (formerly Archdiocese of Glasgow Community Social Services).

The author would finally like to record his grateful thanks to Helen, Cathy and Michael.

He would like to dedicate this book to the memory of his brother John, who suffered from a severe illness that was little understood and for which little appropriate help was available.

Preface

This book is based on work which the author has undertaken in the area of risk assessment and management with a wide range of managers and practitioners including social workers, nurses both community- and hospital-based, health visitors, care workers and independent sector staff. Service users and informal carers have also been involved. The work has covered all key areas, from children and young people, and adults in the fields of health, social care and housing, covering topics such as care of older people, physical disabililty, mental health, learning disability, homelessness and criminal justice.

It is also based on research reviews of the literatures on risk and field research conducted by the author. Some of this material has been published in a chapter for a collection *Risk Assessment in Social Care and Social Work*, edited by Phyllida Parsloe, in the Research Highlights in Social Work series (Jessica Kingsley Publishers). It has been updated for the purposes of this book.

The author's interest in risk was stimulated by the challenge of training in remote and rural locations such as Western Isles and Shetland in the early 1990s. A training course, Risk Taking and Choice for Vulnerable People, was devised and run, later turning into a course on Risk Assessment and Risk Management, which was staged in many varied locations. The author has also worked with the topic of risk as a developmental consultant in the field of health promotion in the UK and international settings, including Eastern Europe. This work has included understanding and addressing risk behaviours in a variety of contexts, including children and young people, HIV/AIDS, prison and mental health.

This book is intended as a guide and a resource for people interested in the topics of risk and risk taking in health and social welfare settings. Readers' comments will be warmly welcomed and can be sent to the author care of the publisher.

Introduction

The topic of 'risk' is an exciting one and interest in it is well established. This is due to a variety of reasons, ranging from the impact of the restructuring of health and community care to professional concerns about the quality of life of people in hospital and community settings. 'Risk Taking' is an idea which will become increasingly important for health and social welfare professionals. However it has to be recognised that risk also poses important dilemmas for professionals and their colleagues, for people who require care, for their families and kin, and for other members of society and their communities.

There is a growing expectation that work in the field of health and social welfare, including health promotion, should involve helping people to have a greater say over their lives and to take more responsibility for their actions. This involves the exercising of choice and will mean that some people will want to take risks in their lives. There is much talk at present of empowerment and the facilitation of choice for vulnerable individuals and communities. Risk provides an innovative and challenging way of bringing about genuine change in the way health and social services are conceived, planned and delivered.

In this book the author examines some of the issues behind these dilemmas and proposes a framework for addressing these issues in a systematic yet person-centred way. The book contains a discussion of risk and risk taking; an analysis of the social construction of risk-taking behaviour; guidance on good practice in risk assessment and management; case studies and examples in the area of risk taking. There is a discussion of the key issues involved in making decisions about risk and some guidelines for improving risk assessment and risk management.

A systematic approach is put forward to help care and other staff, vulnerable individuals and their families. This is called PRAMS – Person-centred Risk Assessment and Management System – and has been used and adapted by a range of different agencies in the field of welfare. In addition, there is a discussion of the effectiveness of training and its limitations; some recent research is put forward in order to throw some light on this topic. The subject of developing skills for professionals and for laypeople is also examined here.

Risk taking is very much a developing topic: it remains under-researched and has yet to be given the priority it deserves. There is no foolproof system of guidance and this statement applies to the guidelines contained here. Indeed, almost by definition, 'risk' cannot be simply quantified and predicted; uncertainty lies at the heart of the enterprise. What the welfare professional can do is systematically to review his or her practice and ensure that he or she takes sensible steps to avoid negligence.

Why has there been such preoccupation with risk of late? The topic has moved to the forefront of our society in various ways: concerns about risks to children facing potential harm, risk to the public from community care cases, but also a broader set of concerns: HIV/AIDS, BSE, Chernobyl, environmental disasters, pollution and accidents. The public perceptions of risks and realities of risk have been the subject of comment; Franklin and others provide a helpful overview of what they see as the 'politics of risk' (Franklin 1998), while other authors such as Joffe (1999) focus on the need to consider emotional responses to such risks. Managing risk has become 'a priority for the health service' (Bowden 1995, p.1). Kemshall *et al.* (1997) claim that the concept of risk is becoming a key organising principle in the social services and probation services.

Some academic commentators have gone as far to claim that we are now living in a 'risk society' (e.g. Beck 1992.) This notion has influenced much recent academic discourse (see e.g. Taylor-Gooby 2001; Duff 2003; Powell and Edwards 2003; Scourfield and Welsh 2003), as will be seen in the first chapter. In Chapter 1 aspects of this discourse will be considered, with a view to considering whether there are implications for policy and practice in health and welfare settings.

For welfare professionals, risk is part of their daily professional lives and has long been so. However recent shifts in policy and legislation in welfare have meant that risk has been moved significantly higher up the agenda. The principle and philosophy of care in the community and of encouraging vulnerable individuals to lead ordinary lives in the community and out of residential and institutional settings is one such example. The rhetoric has to do with choice and taking risks but the reality has meant pressures on practitioners and managers at the front line.

At the same time as the rhetoric has increased, practice has lagged behind, for various reasons. There is also in residential and hospital settings a search for improved quality of care, involving greater individual say over choices, with implications for the taking of risks. The emergence of the clinical governance agenda has meant that both policymakers and practitioners in the NHS are increasingly required to think about risk; as Suckling, Ferris and Price note, 'the continuing identification, assessment and management of risks are key themes for clinical governance' (2003, p.138).

There have been, moreover, developments in field social work, which have combined to push the topics of risk and risk assessment to the fore. In Scotland for example, these drivers include the evolution of an honours social work degree and educational standards, the issuing of guidance by the new Social Services Council and the pressures on social work in the wake of recent tragedies in Lothian and the Borders (see for e.g. Scottish Executive 2003; Scottish Social Services Council 2003; Scottish Social Work Services Inspectorate 2004). Social service employers are being advised to fashion written policies on risk assessment as a matter of priority (Scottish Social Services Council 2003). Some Scottish illustrations are used throughout this text, since Scotland is taking a progressive lead on several fronts in social policy (see also Titterton 2000). National care standards are being developed that are raising a standard, so to speak, north of the border in favour of a risk approach (Scottish Executive 2004b, 2004c, 2004d). Mention is made of other parts of the UK; for example, in Northern Ireland guidance has been issued to social care workers (Northern Ireland Social Care Council 2002) that explicitly raises the topics of rights and risk taking, topics which are examined in depth in this book.

In this book, the author sets out to explore the dilemmas of risk, to look at its conceptualisation and definitions: he considers why it is important and he attempts to examine issues of good practice in risk assessment and management. Some key dilemmas for professionals, carers and users are explored and some case studies are provided. A model, the PRAMS approach (or Person-centred Risk and Management System), is outlined as a framework for risk decision making.

First, the concepts of 'risk' and 'risk-taking' are examined, along with preceptions of these crucial notions; definitions of these notions are put forward and used throughout the discussion in this text. Recent developments in thinking about risk are also considered. In Chapter 2 the issues of rights, responsibilities and the law are examined: these provide the essential context which welfare professionals have to work within. The thorny issue of restraint in relation to risk taking is also discussed.

Next, the notion of a welfare dilemma is explored and there is a look at some practical examples of risk-taking situations; some preliminary steps for weighing up the risks involved are considered. In the following chapters a more systematic approach for risk decision making is presented. Chapter 4 sets out the PRAMS model and goes on to deal with key principles and policies for risk taking. A systematic approach to risk assessment in provided in Chapter 5, along with a review of the relevant literature. The management of risk is tackled in Chapter 6 and key steps are presented. In Chapter 7, assessment and management are linked together within the PRAMS framework. The effectiveness of training for welfare professionals is examined in Chapter 8, along with the kinds of skills which both practitioners and lay people require for risk taking.

Finally, concluding thoughts are presented on the way forward for a progressive and enlightened approach to risk taking in the field of welfare. Some key messages for policymakers, managers, practitioners, users and informal carers, educators and researchers are spelled out. Appendix 1 provides a note on assessing risk of harm and danger in health and social care settings, using the examples of child protection and sex offenders; Appendix 2 outlines a sample risk assessment and management plan; Appendix 3 contains some case studies relating to welfare dilemmas and risk decision; and Appendix 4 contains a note on health and safety issues.

Chapter 1

What is Risk and Risk Taking?

Introduction

One of the major changes in health and social welfare of late is the growing emphasis on risk and the development of a risk-taking approach in working with vulnerable people. In this chapter the concepts of 'risk' and 'risk taking' are examined. Different perceptions of risk and understandings of these concepts are also considered. It is evident that conceptions of these notions have been changing and it is useful to chart some of these changes, as far as they affect practice in health and social care, and to identify some of the key influences on these shifts. A positive view of risk is argued for, one which promotes the idea of risk as an essential ingredient for improving the quality of life.

First of all, the literature is reviewed and the development of academic and practical understandings of the concepts of 'risk' and 'risk taking' is described. A definition is then put forward, based on the consideration of the arguments contained within the literature and one which resonates with professionals' perceptions of the issues. Then recent thinking on these notions, as reflected in recent studies, is examined and some of the pressing issues which arise for welfare professionals and vulnerable people are considered.

Risk and welfare professionals

There are numerous pressures on welfare professionals to go for a 'safety first approach' rather than a 'risk-taking approach' in their work with clients. The pressures on a profession such as nursing have been discussed by various writers, including Crosland (1992); Young (1994); Cook and Procter (1998); and Alaszewski, Harrison and Manthorpe (1998). Cook and Procter point to the problem created by the 'vague professional guidance about reasonable risk taking' which nurses receive (1998, p.279). The tensions this creates are reflected in the new Code of Professional Conduct for nurses, for example, in directivies concerning 'protecting and supporting [the] health' of individuals, and providing 'safe and competent care' (Nursing and Midwifery Council 2002).

These tensions have been inherited from the way directives in the former Code were interpreted (UKCC 1992, 1996). The Code has in the past been used to justify the premium which nurses have traditionally placed upon safety. However writers such as Crosland, Cook and Procter and Alaszewski *et al.* argue that the Code does allow for the empowerment of patients and service users. As Cook and Procter write, it 'also justifies the incorporation of risk taking into clinical practice if the intended outcome is the patient's best interest' (1998, p.279).

This creates a dilemma for nurses, since the Code appeared to justify practice which emphasises supervision and safety on the one hand, and practice which promotes patient autonomy and independence on the other. This fundamental dilemma can, as Cook has perceptively written elsewhere, lead to nurses 'avoiding risk taking altogether' (1996, p.12). Alaszewski *et al.* (1998) have considered the preparation of nurses for risk assessment and management, finding little evidence of systematic work, with views of risk that differed according to the types of service user involved; this study will be referred to again.

However, such codes are not set in tablets of stone: they need to change and reflect the search for better practice within the nursing profession. An example is given in Chapter 3 of a group of nurses who have tried to develop risk-taking practice within the framework laid down by the UKCC. Social workers as a profession in the UK now at last have Social Care Councils (Social Services Council in Scotland). Social workers have to work within a looser professional framework, which at present consists of legislation and policies laid down by the councils who are responsible for the regulation of practice. This framework is examined in Chapters 2 and 4. Nonetheless, social workers face major dilemmas in the course of their professional practice, as will be emphasised throughout this book.

Apart from the pressures generated by concerns over regulation and professional ethics, there are other pressures on care workers from families, carers and other professionals. Care workers and nurses come to place an absolute priority on safety; their fear is that they will be seen as bad workers or to have failed in their role if a person is injured or injures himself/herself while under their care. This leads to the attitude that vulnerable people need to be protected from activities which may be dangerous, and leads in turn to an emphasis on the use of restraint. The use of restraint is widespread and can be subtle as well as obvious (this point is considered again in the next chapter).

This has often led to the adoption of the 'safety first approach' in the health and social services. As one care worker has noted: 'We're often expected to simply "wrap people up in cotton wool" – to keep them safe and sound, away from any possible harm' (training participant, Shetland). The problem with this sort of 'safety first' approach is:

- it ignores the other needs of vulnerable people
- it denies them the right to choice and self-determination
- it leads to a loss of a sense of self-esteem and respect
- it can lead to a form of institutionalisation with the loss of individuality, volition and an increase in dependence
- at its worst, it can lead to the abuse of vulnerable people.

This approach also has a questionable legal basis, for example in the case of the restraint of an individual, as will be seen in the following chapter. The cost of a 'safety first' approach in terms of the loss of self-care skills, dignity, self-worth and levels of functioning – and independence – can be a heavy one. Moreover it is possible to argue that caring practice based on this approach is counter to good practice. Practitioners have a responsibility to attend to physical, psychological and emotional well-being.

As the nurses who run V Ward at Seacroft Hospital have written, '"total safety" can only exist in an environment of "total control": such an approach would deny people "basic and important human rights: the right to choice, the right to self-determination, the right to privacy, the right to take risks"' (Nursing Development Unit Seacroft Hospital, n.d.). Good health, they suggest, can only be enjoyed in 'an environment which promotes happiness through respect for the dignity and rights of each individual'.

Professionals working with vulnerable people must be prepared to accept the challenge of finding imaginative answers to the problem of the balance between danger and safety. The discussion in this book promotes the development of a 'risk-taking approach' which:

- celebrates the taking of risks as a way of enhancing people's lives

- recognises the importance of psychological and emotional needs, as well as physical needs

- promotes choice and autonomy for the individual

- values the individual, irrespective of whether they live in community or institutional settings

- promotes the rights of vulnerable people and their carers, while accepting that these will sometimes be in conflict.

One of the most difficult things to achieve is the shifting of ingrained professional attitudes. The dominance of the safety-first approach in health and social care can be challenged however. Some examples of welfare professionals who have attempted to change professional and lay attitudes are considered later in this text.

Defining and conceptualising 'risk'

Ideas about risk can be traced back through history. One derivation for the word for 'risk' is, Alison Norman (1988) suggests, from the Greek word 'rhiza' for cliff. This refers to the hazardous journeys undertaken by sailors in Ancient Greece, out of the safety of their home port through the potentially treacherous waters around the coasts, and at the mercy of the sea gods and goddesses. The challenges of sailing in such waters are captured by ancient Greek writers, as in the story of Odysseus, who was a great adventurer and voyager. This is an evocative notion and helps to capture the double-sided meaning of the term: the sailors face potential hazards in setting out, but there are rewards for them when they reach the other parts of the Mediterranean, where they exchange goods and reap the benefit of having taken the risk. This can be a handy metaphor when thinking about risk taking and vulnerable people, especially for trainers.

For some authors, risk has always been central to professions like social work (Alaszewski *et al.* 1998; Brearley 1982; Manthorpe *et al.* 1995, p.20; Parton 1996) and to the health care professions (Heyman 1998). For others, risk remains a contested and multifaceted concept (Stevenson 1999b). One problem is that 'risk' in the care of vulnerable people is typically taken to mean the threat to the well-being or welfare of the individual, their relatives and members of the public and staff. The concept is often interpreted as dealing with the probability of an unfortunate incident occurring. Such incidents result from a conjunction of circumstances which may have harmful consequences. According to writers such as East (1995), the likelihood of such an incident occurring represents its risk.

Perceptions of risk have been changing however. Two influential writers deserve to be highlighted in this respect. The first is Alison Norman, whose work has helped to redefine the relation between risk and rights and has challenged ageism in work with older people. A key development has been the changing perception that risk is 'not, as it is often taken to be, an evil in itself' (Norman 1988, p.82). According to Norman, people take risks every moment of their lives, 'weighing the likely danger of a course of action against the likely gain' (1988, p.82). However as Norman (1980, 1988) has noted, this negative view of risk can also be accompanied by stereotypes and prejudices about old age and old people.

In her seminal text, *Rights and Risk*, published in 1980, she raised some core issues to do with civil liberty in old age. One of the key questions posed was: 'How does one balance the risks of institutionalisation (of older persons) against the risks of remaining independent?' (p.13). Here the focus was on older people and their rights, with a strong plea for rights to be respected. These are themes which were later developed in her research into the provision of longstay care for people with severe dementia (Norman 1987). While the 1980 document and the latter research provided food for thought, little in the way of guidance was provided for professionals.

This was a challenge taken up by Paul Brearley, who has written extensively on social work with older people. In his writings (e.g. 1979, 1982) he has been particularly influential in shaping professional views of risk and in providing a framework for understanding and assessing it. Again Brearley takes as his starting point the critique of ageism. He develops a cogent argument for letting older people take gambles; risk taking should be recognised as important for the quality of life. This applies to all contexts of living, whether residential or non-residential. Brearley explicitly rejected the conflation of the term 'risk' with 'hazard' in an influential analysis (Brearley 1982; Carson 1995; Pilgrim and Rogers 1996).

Questions of individual risk and protection present complex problems. The duty of the practitioner to protect the older person is not clear, he or she contends. He or she has then to take into account the possibility of danger to his or her own personal and professional reputation, as well as the potential danger to others, and then to the person perceived to be 'at risk'. Brearley argued that better analytical tools were required by practitioners, ones which would allow for assessing hazards, dangers and strengths of a particular situation; thus the risks of action or inaction could be properly weighed up. However some of the assumptions underlying Brearley's own framework have been criticised by Macdonald and Macdonald (1999). Brearley's pioneering work in the assessment of risk is returned to in Chapter 5.

The Centre for Policy on Ageing has been a lively source of commentary on the issue of risk. It was commissioned by the Department of Trade and Industry Consumer Safety Unit to carry out a study into aspects of risk taking and safety for older people; this was published under the title *Living Dangerously* by Deirdre Wynne-Harley (1991). This took up themes from earlier work done under the auspices of the Centre for Policy on Ageing, including the discussion document by Norman (1980) and *Home Life*, which set out a code of practice for residential care (Centre for Policy on Ageing 1984). This emphasised the right of the individual to choice and risk taking in whatever setting they lived in. This work was endorsed as guidance by the Department of Health and Social Security and has since been updated (Centre for Policy on Ageing 1996, 1999).

For the *Living Dangerously* study, 150 interviews were conducted with individuals and groups of people aged over 60, and further questionnaires given to another 80 persons, most of whom were living independently. The study sought 'to examine risk taking in the context of daily life' (Wynne-Harley 1991, p.2), using information from the interviews and questionnaires, and views were sought from policy makers and practitioners in health, social welfare and safety, as well as families as supporters of older people. In the study, the concept of 'voluntary risk taking' was unpacked. A distinction was drawn between 'involuntary risk' which might result from a wide variety of sources, including 'from failures in any of a range of services' (1991, p.1). On the other hand:

> voluntary risk taking can only occur when the risks have been identified, enabling individuals to make personal choices about types and levels of risk which are appropriate in certain situations. This then becomes an informed decision. (1991, p.4)

Early discussions with the sample of older persons showed that they tended to hold images which conformed to stereotypes and media images: risk was rarely seen as a 'corollary of choice' which could influence the quality of life. However, by the end of the study half the sample saw risk taking as an important element in lifestyle and nearly half saw risk taking as justified to maintain independence in old age. In her study of the risks older people can face, Wynne-Harley writes: 'Risks and risk taking are commonly seen in a negative light. For example, a thesaurus identifies risk with hazard, menace, peril and danger' (1991, p.1; see also Douglas 1992 and Prins 1996). Equally it can be argued that an 'over-cautious life style can bring its own hazards', so an appropriate balance between risk and safety is desirable (1991, p.1).

Like Norman and Brearley, Wynne-Harley identifies ageist attitudes as a key problem militating against the rights of older people. Many old people have low expectations and a low sense of worth. They share the prevalent negative attitudes to old age. In doing this, they may 'accept the right of those who are younger to make decisions for them, to reduce their autonomy, to eliminate choice and risk from their lives' (1991, p.27). The report concluded that 'reasonable, informed and calculated risk taking plays an important part in contributing to the quality of life for young and old; this is a matter of choice, demonstrating an individual's right to self-determination and autonomy' (1991, p.29).

This theme was taken up by another valuable report, issued this time by Counsel and Care, *What If They Hurt Themselves*, published in 1992. This was a discussion document on the uses and abuses of restraint in residential care and nursing homes for older people. The concern from which this report grew had its origins in visits by Counsel and Care's advice workers to all registered private and voluntary residential care and nursing homes in the Greater London area. The workers reported that they saw a 'great deal of restraint in daily use in homes' (1992, p.3) and were worried about the low quality of life available to someone whose movement was perpetually restricted in the alleged interests of well-being. The report provided examples and tackled the issue of restraint. The restraints in residential settings were found to include:

- individual physical restraint on movement
- physical restraints to circulation in and beyond the building
- drugs
- supervision and observation
- institutional, professional and cultural attitudes
- financially related methods.

Many recommendations were made, including this one aimed at managers of homes: in the contract and care plan for each resident there should be specific reference to the degree of appropriate restraint and risk for that individual. Carers and residents wherever possible should agree such points, which should be regularly reviewed.

The aim was to expand for wider discussion some of the issues raised by the visits: 'the need sometimes to accept the risk of not restraining, and some positive alternatives or at least some more acceptable forms of restraint' (1992, p.4). The authors of the report argued that the lack of widespread professional discussion has led to a 'passive acceptance that restraint is generally acceptable, indeed good caring practice in any situation' (p.4). A key dilemma was posed: what is more important: institutional compliance or personal protection of individuals? That debate continues to this day, particularly in the field of mental health. *What if They Hurt Themselves* usefully raised the idea that principles are needed, along with a framework. This is addressed again in Chapters 4 and 7. The report concluded that 'risk taking' should be seen as part of living at all stages of life' (p.24); the complete removal of risk from people's lives should be seen as unacceptable. Responsible risk taking was advocated. This was a good attempt to raise complex issues for broader debate. It did not succeed in resolving difficult and fraught areas raised by the findings and offered general recommendations but not detailed guidance.

This commitment by Counsel and Care to the idea of risk taking was taken up by a campaign which built on the 1992 report. Funding was obtained from the Mental Health Foundation to finance a project, *The Right To Take Risks*, a pack providing a classification of restraint, policies and guidelines and some training material (Counsel and Care 1993). Life is full of risks, the authors noted; risk taking 'adds a sparkle' to people's lives (p.1). This pack again set out general principles and some valuable points. It represents a fitting culmination to the campaign by Counsel and Care concerning risk taking. However, it was set at a very general level and only a rudimentary framework was provided.

Shifts within the academic literature

There have been perceptible shifts in the way risk is perceived in the academic literature, which has given rise to something which might be called the 'risk paradigm'. Two authors have been particularly influential here. The first of these is Mary Douglas (e.g. 1992), who contends that perceptions of risk will vary from society to society and from person to person. Risk, in other words, is essentially a social construction. Each person and each social group sees risks differently and reacts differently, according to their cultural and social structural locations. Using the example of AIDS, she showed how perceptions of the risks varied in relation to the degree of social integration and acceptance of cultural norms by individuals and by minority communities (Douglas and Calvez 1990). Thus the knowledge base and authority of 'establishment medicine' concerning HIV infection and contamination were rejected by dissenting minorities, including members of the gay community.

For writers like Douglas, risk has become a central category for understanding contemporary society and this is the defining feature of our second author, Ulrich Beck. In his book *Risk Society*, published originally in German in 1992, Beck provided a major analysis of the relationship between risk and society. This text was translated by the sociologist Scott Lash for a British audience and soon began to have a definite impact on the deliberations of some social scientists. Beck argued that modern society had entered a phase where some people are more affected than others by the distribution and growth of risks. Beck has a very negative understanding of 'risk', by which he means primarily dangers posed by the sort of accident that took place at the Chernobyl nuclear reactor in Russia, which had both local and global consequences. The social distribution of these kinds of risks, which include pollution and toxins, replaces the inequality of wealth as the central problem of the new age. He claims his idea of the 'risk society' conveys a new conception of 'non-industrial' society': we have to think afresh about the world we now live in. Paradoxically, the more we have tried to control the world, the more uncertain it becomes. This theory has had an influence on writers like Giddens (1998) and on the Economic and Social Research Council (ESRC), who funded a research programme on risk. However this was mostly about risk conceived largely as scientific risk, with less of a concern with social services (though two projects on this topic were funded).

Giddens and Beck point to misunderstandings that occur when old concepts are used to describe new situations: however, both writers use the term 'risk' indiscriminately. Giddens accepts that risk always has a negative connotation 'since it refers to the chance of avoiding an unwanted outcome' but that it can be often seen in a positive light: 'successful risktakers, whether in exploration, in business or mountaineering, are widely admired' (1998, p.27). He proposes that we need to distinguish risk from hazard, something which Brearley proposed 20 years previously. He then claims that the first two hundred years of industrial society were dominated by 'external risk' or risk of events which might strike individuals unexpectedly but which happened regularly and often enough to a whole population to be broadly predictable, and so insurable (p.27). Here private and public insurance, as in the welfare state, has a role. However, 'manufactured risk' which is risk 'created by the very progression of science and technology' (p.27) establishes a new risk environment of which we have little previous experience. In this scenario we do not really know what the risks are and cannot predict them. As Coote writes, the risk paradigm 'suggests that we live in an uncertain world where we cannot control or predict accurately what will happen to us' (1998, p.124).

This debate is useful for us in that it calls for fresh ways of looking at society and current issues; we are all members of the 'risk society' (Beck 1992, 1998). Risk is being redefined as part of everyday discourse, in a way which challenges rational scientific assumptions about prediction and control of the natural and social worlds (Lash *et al.* 1996; Dingwall 2000; Parton 1998). Where the debate has been less helpful is in the way that it is conducted at a very abstract level, with sweeping assertions about 'postmodern society' or 'late modernity' taking the place of careful and well-researched argument. What has been missing has been theoretical development, particularly the articulation of a positive conception of risk and the formulation of middle range concepts: in other words, concepts that link the grand theory beloved of social scientists with empirical matters and practical concerns.

An additional difficulty arises from the broad socio-cultural sweep of this debate. For authors such as Joffe (1999), there has been a failure to incorporate social psychological insights into how people respond to risk; she contends that emotional factors must play a major role in how people react, particularly in relation to explaining how people cope with living in the 'risk society'. One field of studies which has attempted to build on insights gleaned from postmodernist theory and to bring in issues for individuals living in what Wilkinson (1996) calls 'unhealthy societies' is that of health promotion (Harrison 2002). Here lively debates have been taking place, where for example it has been claimed there are clear affinities between postmodernism and health promotion, since health should be construed as a multiply determined and multidimensional concept (Webb and Wright 2000, citing Rubenstein *et al.* 1998). The risk discourse in its various forms has received much attention from researchers and writers and aspects of this work are referred to in relevant sections throughout the book. The health promotion literature is contributing much to changing understandings of 'risk' and 'risk taking', for instance in areas of work with young people and with topics such the misuse of alcohol and drugs and prevention of HIV/AIDS (see e.g. Health Education Authority 1998). Again this work will be referred to later.

Despite the theoretical problems, the work of writers like Douglas and Beck indicates that there is a need to think carefully about the concept of 'risk' and particularly about the language which welfare professionals and others use. The practical aspects of the definition and clarification of the concept should be clear: how we deal with a social problem is influenced by how we define that problem (Manning 1987). Clarity of language is essential yet the term 'risk' is often used indifferently at best and carelessly at worst. People often deploy terms like 'children at risk' or 'elderly at risk' when what is really meant is that they are 'at risk of harm'. For people to grow and develop as creative and autonomous beings, they have to engage with risk. The notion of risk taking as a 'right' has been discussed by Counsel and Care (1993) for older people and has been explored further by Harrer and Thom (1997) in the case of older persons and alcohol. The implications of this have still to be thought through, as will be seen in the following chapter.

More recently, the literature has been preoccupied with pondering on the significance of the 'risk society', particularly in the twenty-first century. Adam, Beck and Van Loon (2000) have called for a 'repositioning of risk' within social theory. The implications for the welfare state have been dwelt on by some writers (e.g. Taylor-Gooby *et al.* 1999; Taylor-Gooby 2001). Others have sought to examine the relationship to 'moral panics' and anxieties about new 'folk devils', building on Cohen's fruitful early analysis of the labelling and stereotyping of threats to societal values (Cohen 1972; Ungar 2001; Hier 2003). Still others have attempted to reconsider issues in child protection in the light of notions about risk society (Houston and Griffiths 2000; Scourfield and Welsh 2003). Risk is seen as a 'centrally defining motif of "late modernity"', for instance, one which governs the relationship between youth and the welfare state (Powell and Edwards 2003, p.90; see also Cieslik and Pollok 2002).

Some academics have focused instead on the displacement of need by risk as a key principle behind changes in public services and have called for social models of risk, which could provide a more empowering approach (Alaszewski *et al.* 1998; Kemshall 2002b; Kemshall *et al.* 1997; Stalker 2003). Quite how the tensions they identify between 'risk versus need' and 'risk management versus empowerment' are to be handled is, however, less than clear in the literature.

The practical effects of risk are still under study: the World Health Organization (WHO), in its latest report on the state of world health for 2002, dedicated substantial space to the topic of risk and its importance for global health (WHO 2002). It is a little unfortunate that risk is defined solely in terms of adverse outcomes for health in the report. It has, however, highlighted risk communication as an issue worth further study by academics and practitioners alike. The 'politics of risk communication' have a distinctive part to play in modern society (Bennett and Calman 2001; Franklin 1998); they shape and some would say distort our perceptions of risk and they impact massively upon the world of the health and social care professional.

A definition of risk and risk taking

A precise definition of 'risk' is called for, and a more balanced one, which emphasises its positive as well as its negative nature. The preliminary explorations of Brearley and Norman have been revived by some of the more recent discussions of risk (Alberg *et al.* 1996; Carson 1995; Manthorpe *et al.* 1997). Risk taking can have beneficial as well as harmful outcomes. A core task that health and social care practitioners face is to identify the types of benefits and harms which may occur, as well as their likelihood. They need to be more specific about the range of factors which affect the likelihood or probability of certain kinds of outcomes. They should also attempt to specify the timescale within which the risk taking activity is intended to take place. A helpful definition of 'risk' has been provided by Alberg and colleagues: *'the possibility of beneficial and harmful outcomes and the likelihood of their occurrence in a stated timescale'* (1996, p.9).

In both the academic and professional literatures 'risk taking' tends to remain undefined. However, in the field of health and social care, clarity is required in the understanding and deployment of terms. Based on the discussion contained in this chapter and building on and refining the work of the Centre for Policy on Ageing (e.g. Wynne-Harley 1991), we can define the concept as follows: *Risk taking is a course of purposeful action based on informed decisions concerning the possibility of positive and negative outcomes of types and levels of risk appropriate in certain situations.* This conceptualisation helps to capture the elements of purpose and objective setting, as well as option appraisal and decision making within set boundaries. The facilitation of choice and delimitation of those boundaries form core components of the professional's task in relation to risk and these themes are picked up in the discussion that follows this chapter.

Various writers have argued that risk taking is all about uncertainty (see particularly Parton 1996, 1998). This leads Heyman to define risk as 'the projection of a degree of uncertainty about the future on to the external world' (1998, p.5). The possible outcomes of a proposed course of activity could in theory be infinite and it is impossible to predict something with absolute certainty. In the complex world of human interaction we should not expect to do so. Instead, the professional art of risk taking lies in the weighing up of likely outcomes and the use of professional judgement, guided by a systematic method of risk assessment and management.

Conclusion

In this chapter conceptions of risk have been reviewed and its importance for welfare professionals and the rest of society have been examined. Some important shifts within professional conceptions of risk taking were charted, along with recent debates within the academic literature. It has been argued here that risk is socially constructed and needs to be understood as involving both positive and negative consequences for the vulnerable individual in welfare settings, within a particular time frame. It is also contended that the definition of risk embracing the stipulation of beneficial and harmful outcomes is essential.

Risk taking, moreover, should be conceived of as purposive action based on informed choices concerning it, in relation to types and levels of risk appropriate in specific situations. The element of uncertainty must however be acknowledged as a core feature of the professional's art; so too is the specification of boundaries for this lack of certainty and these features are discussed in later chapters.

In the next chapter, issues to do with rights, responsibilities and the law with respect to risk taking for vulnerable people and their carers are considered.

Chapter 2

Rights, Responsibilities and the Law

Introduction

Risk taking in health and welfare settings does not take place in a vacuum. It is best understood within the context of the rights and responsibilities of vulnerable people, their carers and the rest of society. In this chapter the author examines the issues raised by the law in relation to risk and risk taking; the discussion then goes on to consider the importance of rights and responsibilities and some fundamental dilemmas in respect of striking an appropriate balance between the two. The issue of restraint in respect of the legal framework and in relation to the taking of risks is also discussed.

Risk taking and the law

In promoting a more positive approach towards the taking of risks, welfare professionals should not fight shy of taking the legal implications of risk decisions into account. As Clements and McDonald note, the 'law is all around us in imposing obligations and granting rights which affect us in every aspect of our lives' (2002, p.3). The application of law involves the consideration of rights, duties, powers and remedies, all of which interconnect in ways which practitioners should try to understand. Brearley (1982) argues that the best protection for the social worker lies in good practice and in recognising the potential of the law for use in dangerous situations. The law protects clients, the worker and the agency too.

Carson (1996) suggests that it is possible to go further and proposes that use can be made of legal concepts and the operation of the legal system to help improve risk decision making and justify decisions. He contends that practitioners can use the concepts of the law and its procedures for their own purposes, before harm occurs. It has to be accepted, however, that the law will not give us direct answers, but it can help provide procedures and frameworks for use by professionals and others in making risk decisions.

Comments made in the training courses run by the author suggest that social workers and other professionals do not feel particularly comfortable with their knowledge of the law and with the legal implications of taking risks: There is a 'cover your back' mentality which gets in the way of creative practice (training participant, Fife); 'often you feel you have to keep looking over your shoulder' (training participant, East Renfrewshire); 'the department is worried about being sued for negligence' (training participany, Dundee). Workers and their managers sometimes hold distorted views of the legal implications of risk taking, particularly over the issue of negligence. These implications tend to be overlooked by writers in the field of risk work. One exception is David Carson (1990, 1996, 1997) who has been attempting to promote the positive side of risk taking and to encourage professionals to use the concepts of the law to justify and improve their risk decisions. He is a critic of negative attitudes among managers and others in the social services. Carson argues that such managers may well find themselves sued for not tackling risks and for not ensuring that their staff are trained. These attitudes lead to defensiveness and unimaginative practice.

However, Carson tends to underestimate the resistance of professionals and managers which may have its roots in cultural and organisational factors, rather than just a lack of clarity about the law. Another author, John Tingle, has more recently examined the issue of clinical negligence and nursing and has argued that the context of the NHS in terms of clinical governance, patient safety and patient empowerment means that nurses and doctors need to acquaint themselves with these changes and develop a better understanding of negligence (Tingle 2002a, 2002b). The Government has plans to issue a clinical negligence White Paper.

One notion, that of a 'duty of care', remains to be adequately explored. Some of the legal considerations arising from patient homicides and the implications for assessment and management of risk have been discussed by Kennedy and Gill (1997). They warn of the danger of defensiveness, particularly if patient-as-plaintiffs cases succeed. The outcome of the Christopher Clunis case which came before the Court of Appeal in 1998 resulted in the turning down of Clunis's application for damages, with no leave for further appeal. Nonetheless, more claims along similar lines will no doubt be put forward for consideration by the courts. A useful discussion of the legal duty of care in relation to nursing is contained in Tingle (2002c, 2002d).

The problems facing risk assessment in a 'climate of litigation' have been explored by Harrison (1997). She argues that there has been a 'seachange' in the attitudes of professionals towards the use of litigation in medicine, and towards the assessment of risk to themselves of an untoward incident. She criticises what she sees as the tendency to develop a new form of institutionalisation, where patients become 'entangled in webs of overcautious surveillance by mental health professionals' and the new bureaucracy arising from the Care Programme Approach and defensive practices (p.37). A similar debate has been taking place in the United States, where concerns about professional duties and responsibilities, litigation and risk assessment in 'managed care' settings have been mounting (Simon 1998). In a similar vein, Scheflin (1998) has argued that risk management needs to take account of the current wave of lawsuits so that mental health professionals can avoid litigation.

Differences within the UK are often overlooked, yet they can be very instructive for policy and legal learning (Titterton 2001). In Northern Ireland, which has an integrated health and social services system, the Government has established a review of mental health and learning disability to consider the reform of mental health legislation, policy and services. A debate has recently developed over the human rights of people with mental health problems and learning disabilities. This includes the issue of capacity and potential human rights violations, as well as the lack of services for those aged under 18 (Davidson, McCallion and Potter 2003). This discussion has been taking place within the context of developing awareness of human rights since the Good Friday Agreement and growing acknowledgement of the need to consider international standards.

The impact of human rights issues has been notable in Northern Ireland, resulting in the setting up of a Human Rights Commission. The other countries of the UK are starting to feel the effect of the rise of human rights issues, with the incorporation of the European Convention on Human Rights into UK law. The Human Rights Act 1998 incorporated most, but not all of the Convention. The Act made it unlawful for any public body to act, either by commission or omission, in a way incompatible with the rights of the Convention as stipulated by its articles. To take one example, Article 5, on the right to liberty and security, could be construed in a way that makes restrictions on vulnerable people a breach of the article; this would embrace the locked-door regimes of residential and other units. In 2000 an order was made to bring the Human Rights Act 1998 into force across the UK (earlier in Scotland).

A new Commission for Equality and Human Rights was proposed in a White Paper in May 2004, to combine the work of the Commission for Racial Equality, the Disability Rights Commission and the Equal Opportunities Commission and take on additional responsibilities in respect of age, sexual orientation and religious belief. For the first time, institutional support will be provided for human rights, to ensure that the latter are placed 'at the heart of public service delivery' (Department of Trade and Industry 2004, p.1). However, a House of Commons Committee has already expressed concern that, in respect of human rights issues, the Commission will only have powers of promotion and not powers of enforcement (House of Commons Health Committee 2004).

It is as yet early days for human rights legislation in the UK context, and judgements in relation to cases brought before the European Court of Human Rights will help shape how such legislation should be interpretated. One possibility for the future may be the rise of actions brought to redress what are perceived as infringements of the rights of service users in respect of risk taking. This is a space worth watching.

Scotland, like Northern Ireland, has a distinctive health and social care system, as well as legal framework, although some of the issues remain the same as in other parts of the UK (Titterton 1991, 2001). The area of mental health law, moreover, provides an instructive example to consider. There were concerns expressed there about the need to revise the Mental Health (Scotland) Act 1984 and the need to tighten up the law around the rights of 'incapable adults' (Law Society of Scotland, Royal College of Psychiatrists, Scottish Division and Scottish Association for Mental Health 1996). In response a committee was set up by the Scottish Executive, charged with reviewing mental health legislation in Scotland; this was in recognition of the significant changes in the way in which mental health services are organised since the Act was passed (Scottish Executive 2001). The Scottish Law Commission (1996) published a report which set out general principles for intervention in the life of someone unable to make decisions for himself or herself and which received a favourable welcome. This report took as its remit the whole of Scots law about decision making for people in this position.

By 'incapable adults' the Commission meant people who are unable to take a decision at a certain time. However, they excluded people admitted to hospital under the Mental Health (Scotland) Act 1984, since they tend not to advocate reform where legislation has been passed. This contrasts with the message of others who have been calling for reform, as noted above. The problem is that the law was 'patchy and piecemeal, with no general principles' (Patrick 1996, p.1). There were gaps in the system and many different remedies can be used, some of them being very old. An example is the 'tutor dative' procedure which is described below.

The report issued by the Lord Chancellor's Department in December 1997 presented the Government's view of what constitutes a 'vulnerable adult', which is a person:

> who is or may be in need of community care services by reason of mental or other disability, age or illness; and who is or may be unable to take care of him or herself, or unable to protect him or herself against significant harm or exploitation.

This definition has been widely used; it was used, for example, in the No Secrets guidance produced by the Government (Department of Health and Home Office 2000). It has been criticised for its assumption of the need of the person for external help and for appearing to exclude those who do not require care services and who can care for themselves. The recent Parliamentary inquiry into elder abuse recommended expanding the definition to take account of this (House of Commons Health Committee 2004, Recommendation 2).

Less controversially, the authors of the report declared that there exists a 'clear need for reform of the law', at least in respect of the situation in England (Lord Chancellor's Department 1997, p.1). The law in this area has "developed in a piecemeal fashion and does not always offer sufficient protection either for mentally incapacitated adults, or for those who look after them" (Lord Chancellor's Department 1997, p.1). The report addressed the issue of protection for people without capacity and vulnerable adults. The consultation paper sought views on a possible framework for providing that protection; the report was based on the work of the Law Commission. Some minor differences can be seen between the work of the Law Commission and the Scottish Law Commission but underlying principles are shared.

The Law Commission had recommended a new statutory definition of incapacity, where there is a presumption against lack of capacity and where capacity is defined in a functional manner (Law Commission 1995, para. 3.23). They also proposed this definition of 'vulnerable person':

A vulnerable person is someone of 16 years or over who:

- is or may be in need of community care services for reasons of mental or other disability, age or illness, and who
- is or may be unable to take care of him or herself, or unable to protect him or herself against significant harm or exploitation.

The Commission also sought to build on the significant harm test included in the Children Act 1989. Harm should be taken to include not only ill-treatment (including sexual abuse and forms of ill-treatment which are not physical) but also 'the impairment of, or an avoidable deterioration in, physical or mental health; and the impairment of physical, intellectual, emotional, social or behavioural development' (1995, p.103). The Commission recommended introducing a duty on social service authorities to make enquiries where they have reason to believe that a vulnerable person in their area is suffering or likely to suffer significant harm or serious exploitation.

However it was not until June 2003 that the Government published a Mental Incapacity Bill, which was subject to scrutiny by Parliament and others. A new Mental Capacity Bill was published in June 2004, based on key principles (Department of Constitutional Affairs 2004). There is a presumption of capacity and a single test is proposed for assessing capacity of an individual to take a particular decision at a particular time.

The Scottish Law Commission received 'widespread acclaim', according to Patrick (1996, p.2) for a 'fair, comprehensive and humane system based on enlightened principles'. It proposed a flexible system of personal and financial guardianship for people unable to manage their own affairs: friends and relations should be encouraged to act as guardians; this would replace guardianship under the Mental Health (Scotland) Act, tutors dative and curator bonis.

On the face of it, many of the recommendations contained in the reports of the Lord Chancellor's Department, the Law Commission and Scottish Law Commission were reasonable ones and they helped to clarify areas which were very muddy. The Scottish Parliament eventually passed an Act on Incapable Adults in 2000. However there is little recognition in any of these reports of the dangers of the overprotection of vulnerable adults. In the years ahead this will be the key challenge: clarification of the law concerning vulnerable and mentally incapacitated adults avoiding statutory measures which would deny such adults and their carers the chance to take risks.

Social workers and other welfare professionals have to operate within a patchy and ill-defined context. There are two issues to consider here. The first is that much of the legislative provision that does exist tends to deal with constraints and restraints on individuals, such as compulsory admission to care. 'Risk', to the extent that it features at all, is largely conceived of in a negative and constraining manner. The statutory framework of rights governing vulnerable adults tends to be defined in a similar manner. For example, there is no clear statutory framework for older people. The problem in the eyes of those who lobby for the rights of older people is that there is no coherent legislative framework for vulnerable adults comparable to that which exists for children. There is nothing equivalent to the Children's Acts, which are based on principles which have been widely agreed and which rely, at least in part, on internationally defined agreements such as the United Nations Convention on the Rights of the Child (Hill and Aldgate 1996).

The second issue is whether there are lessons from the field of children's rights, legislation and risk for the field of vulnerable adults. Some people have attempted to draw out messages from child protection for the protection of older people from abuse or for mental health risk management (Bond 1998; Stevenson 1996, 1999a). It is important to be clear about the kinds of risk models imported from the area of child abuse. Attempting to protect older people from risky situations would be contrary to the risk taking model. Indeed, it is possible to go further and criticise some child protection approaches as limited in their narrow focus on risk as 'danger'. The rights and risks for older people and other vulnerable adults have to be considered, before there is a rush to accept an all-embracing framework for the 'protection' of adults.

Next we consider the legislative framework, and issues to do with the 'duty of care', negligence and legal action, as well as managers' liability. We then go on to look at restraint, the question of rights and the justifying of decisions.

The legislative framework

No statutory framework for 'risk taking' exists as such. For vulnerable adults, there is a body of community care law in the United Kingdom, which does not yet amount to a coherent legislative package. There are instead a number of relevant provisions in different Acts passed at different times for different purposes. There are, moreover, a body of legal rules contained in a variety of statutory instruments, directions from the Secretaries of State and circulars issued by the Department of Health, Scottish Executive, Welsh Office and Northern Ireland Office (for England and Wales, see Clements 1996 and McDonald 2004; for the Scottish position see McKay and Patrick 1995; see also Fabb and Guthrie 1997 on social work and the law in Scotland). These, along with the Codes of Practice issued by the Government, form what some call 'quasi-legislation'. Writing about community care law in England and Wales, Clements writes that it is a 'hotch-potch of conflicting statutes, which have been enacted over a period of 50 years; each statute reflects the different philosophical attitudes of its time' (Clements 1996, p.10). The legal frameworks in respect of working with children and sex offenders are considered separately in Appendix I.

The principal Acts of Parliament in relation to vulnerable adults in England and Wales are as follows:

- Public Health Acts 1931 and 1961 includes ss. 83–85, which give power to enter and clean premises.

- National Assistance Act 1948, e.g., 29 to promotes the welfare of people with disabilities; ss. 21–26 cover the duty to provide residential accommodation for vulnerable adults; and s. 47 allows for the removal of a vulnerable person living in unsanitary conditions and suffering from neglect.

- Chronically Sick and Disabled Persons Act 1970, e.g., s. 2 puts a duty on local authorities to meet the needs of people in relation to s.29 of the above act.

- Health Services and Public Health Act 1968, e.g., s. 45 enables local authorities to promote the welfare of old people.

- Housing Act 1996 includes pt. 7, which places a duty on local authorities to house homeless persons with a priority need e.g. due to physical disability.

- National Health Service Act 1977 includes sched. 8, which enables local authorities to make arrangements to prevent illness, provide aftercare and provide home help and laundry services.

- Mental Health Act 1983 – this complex legislation is under review. S. 2 provides for compulsory admission for assessment; s. 3 for compulsory admission for treatment; ss. 7–11 cover guardianship; s.13(4) places a duty on local authorities to provide an approved social worker where required; and s. 177 provides for after care treatment by local authorities, jointly with health authorities.

- Disabled Persons (Services, Consultation and Representation) Act 1986 provides for the written assessment of need for people with disabilities.

- NHS and Community Care Act 1990, e.g., s. 47 provides a framework for all assessments of people who may be in need of community care services, with the local authority as lead agency.

- Disability Discrimination Act 1995 outlaws discrimination against an individual on the grounds of his or her disability.

- Community Care (Direct Payments) Act 1996 enables local authorities to make cash payments to vulnerable adults to arrange their own care.

- Data Protection Act 1998 covers how information about people is used; all organisations that hold or process personal data must comply.

- Human Rights Act 1998 is based on the European Convention on Human Rights and was brought into force in 2000.

- Disability Rights Commission Act 1999 covers the setting up of the Disability Rights Commission.

- Care Standards Act 2000 was implemented in April 2002 and replaces the Registered Homes Act 1984. It established a National Care Standards Commission and General Social Care Council. This act also makes provision for:
  - the protection of children and vulnerable adults
  - national register of persons unsuitable to work with vulnerable adults
  - registration, regulation and training of social care workers.

- Health and Social Care (Community Health and Standards) Act 2003 covered the establishment of the Commission for Social Care Inspection and Commission for Healthcare Audit and Inspection

- Mental Capacity Bill – a Bill was published in June 2003 (originally entitled Mental Incapacity Bill), scrutinised by a Parliamentary Committee; the Government published a response in February 2004 and a new Bill in June 2004.

- Mental Health Bill – a Bill was published in June 2003, scrutinised by a Parliamentary Committee and the Government published a response in February 2004.

- Disability Discrimination Bill.

Other acts could be mentioned, for example in respect of measures available for the protection of vulnerable adults. There is also a large body of circulars and guidance, such as the Government's No Secrets document, requiring the development and implementation of multiagency policies and procedures (Department of Health and Home Office 2000). This document set out a definition of abuse as follows: 'Abuse is a violation of an individual's human and civil rights by any other person or persons' (Department of Health and Home Office 2000, para. 2.5).

Nonetheless, the impression gleaned from this short review of legislation should be clear: there is a considerable array of legislative measures available but they still constitute a 'hotchpotch', to use Clements's description. Some complex areas, such as legislation covering people with mental health problems, have been under active review since 1998 and are subject to intense debate and criticism. The Mental Capacity

Bill was mentioned earlier and is presently before Parliament; it is designed to reform the law in respect of the decision-making process for those unable to make decisions for themselves (Department of Constitutional Affairs 2004). A new offence of ill-treatment or wilful neglect of a person lacking capacity is proposed by the bill. A new Mental Health Bill is also before Parliament; this sets out the safeguards and procedures for the treatment of someone for his or her mental disorder without his or her consent. As well as defining procedures for assessment and treatment, the Bill provides some safeguards and support for patients so that their voice can be heard. People will be treated compulsorily only if they meet a particular definition of mental disorder and a set of 'relevant conditions'. The new Act will apply equally to Wales but a separate Code of Practice is being drawn up and the Welsh Assembly will be responsible for implementation (Department of Health 2004c).

There have also been lively discussions north of the border about mental health legal reform, as well as about capacity and decision making; these are discussed on the following pages.

In Scotland, the law in relation to vulnerable adults is similarly a mixture of legislative measures. The principal Acts of Parliament are as follows.

- National Assistance Act 1948, e.g., s. 47 covers compulsory treatment and s. 48(2) covers protection of property.

- Social Work (Scotland) Act 1968 empowers local authorities to promote social welfare and includes obligations to provide residential accommodation and domiciliary and laundry services (s. 14).

- Mental Health (Scotland) Act 1984 includes ss. 17, 24, and 26, which govern compulsory admission to mental hospital, as well as guardianship.

- Disabled Persons (Services, Consultation and Representation) Act 1986 includes s. 1 and s. 2, which govern advocacy and representation, and were not implemented.

- NHS and Community Care Act 1990 added ten new provisions to the Social Work (Scotland) Act 1968, e.g., s. 12a where local authorities have a duty to carry out assessments for anyone who appears to be in need of 'community care services'.

- Mental Health (Patients in the Community) Act 1995 introduced Community Care Orders.

- Carers (Recognition and Services) Act 1995 introduced right of assessment of carers.

- Disability Discrimination Act 1995 was intended to outlaw discrimination against an individual on the grounds of his or her disability.

- Direct Payments Act 1996 introduced the power for local authorities to make direct payments to certain groups of vulnerable persons.

- Data Protection Act 1998 deals with how information about people is used. All Scottish organisations that hold or process personal data must comply.

- Human Rights Act 1998 was brought into force in the UK in 2000 and incorporates the European Convention on Human Rights into Scots law in relation to the acts of public bodies.

- Adults With Incapacity Act 2000 was presented to the Scottish Parliament in March as part of its new legislative programme.

- Regulation of Care (Scotland) Act 2001 established the Scottish Commission for the Regulation of Care, the Scottish Social Services Council and National Care Standards.

- Community Care and Health (Scotland) Act 2002 provided free personal and nursing care for older persons.

- Mental Health (Care and Treatment) (Scotland) Act 2003 reformed law on compulsory treatment and introduced right of access to independent advocacy services.

There have also been concerns expressed about the need to revise the Mental Health (Scotland) Act 1984 (Law Society for Scotland *et al.* 1996) and to tighten up the law around the rights of 'incapable adults'; the Scottish Law Commission published a report on the latter (Scottish Law Commission 1996). The Adults With Incapacity Act 2000 is one outcome of these concerns. A committee under the chairmanship of Bruce Millan was established to review the Act and a report of its review was made available in 2001 (Scottish Executive 2001). The Mental Health (Care and Treatment) (Scotland Act) 2003 is the result of debates generated by the Millan Review and discussions around compulsory treatment in the community, a debate largely started south of the border. Another recent Act, the Regulation of Care (Scotland) Act 2001, also has major implications for social service providers not just in mental health but across the board for other care groups.

A comparative look at the four countries of the UK – England, Wales, Scotland and Northern Ireland – reveals interesting divergences but also some common elements (see e.g. Titterton 2000; 2001). One shared feature is the emergence of a regulation agenda, marked by a top-down approach to standard setting, inspection and audit, albeit ameliorated by some consultation of service users and their carers. The public purse in all four countries has been used to fund the growth of regulatory mechanisms, rather than invested in a bottom-up approach to empower frontline staff, users and informal carers through skills development, training and support to develop risk-taking approaches. Whether this has been a wise investment remains to be seen. In the meantime it is to be hoped that risk taking is not discouraged by narrow constructions of the regulation agenda.

The legislative framework has been developing rapidly over the last few years in all four countries of the UK, particularly in the fields of mental health and the rights of children and vulnerable adults. Nonetheless, there still remain patchy and ill-defined areas that social workers and other welfare professionals have to operate within, where key skills for decision making have to be developed. This is discussed further in the next chapter and in Chapter 8.

Duty of care, breach of statutory duty, negligence and legal action

In order to develop a risk approach, it is important to place issues to do with litigation and negligence into perspective. Some professionals and managers express concern about being sued, for example where a risk decision has had an adverse outcome. Such concerns can lead to a 'safety first' approach and to a marked reluctance to countenance risk taking. Definitions of 'negligence' and 'neglect' are important too (Stevenson 1996). As Clements and McDonald state, the enforcement of duties by an 'action for breach of statutory duty' might be thought to be commonly available, but 'this is not in fact the case', 'most statutory duties have been seen as "target duties"; this means that they are seen as existing for the benefit of the population as a whole, or a specified group within it, rather than for the benefit of individuals within that group' (2002, p.61). The discussion that follows is based on considerations by Clements and McDonald (2002); Carson (1996); Giliker and Beckwith (2000); McHale and Tingle (2001); McKay and Patrick 1995; Rogers (2002); and Tingle (2002a, 2002b, 2002c, 2002d).

There is no law of 'risk' or 'risk taking' as such; risk is not a legal concept. The key concept under the law is 'negligence'. Actions for breach of statutory duty and actions in negligence are private law matters where compensation by way of damages is sought by individuals. A negligence action might arise due to a risk decision which 'resulted' in harm. Even where a negligence action is not a viable course, a risk decision might be involved in the following:

- complaints procedure
- formal inquiry
- disciplinary proceedings.

The key issue is whether the worker acted in a manner comparable to how others would have acted. So the main question is: would a responsible body of fellow professionals have made the same decision and can this be demonstrated?

A negligence action must pass some demanding tests, as outlined below:

1. Negligence and the 'duty of care'

If there is no legal duty of care, no legal action regarding negligence is applicable. The notion of 'duty of care' has not really been explored by the literature or tested by the law in the UK. The law says that whenever someone takes responsibility for another person, he or she should do so carefully. Difficulties can arise since the law is not always clear about when there is a duty to take care. As yet, no single general principle covering the duty of care has been spelled out by the courts. However, there have developed formulations from cases which have come before the courts. These can be summarised as:

(a)   The worker must owe a duty of care to the injured party.

(b)   There are limits to this (there must be a 'sufficiently proximate relationship' between the parties).

(c)   The court has discretion, e.g. policy implications are taken into account. It has to be 'fair, just and reasonable' for a duty of care to be imposed by the court, in the light of policy considerations which the court is concerned with.

2. Breach of 'standard of care'

(a)   The court can decide the standard is too low.

(b)   The court will examine how and why a decision was made.

(c)   The key question is: would fellow professionals agree?

3. Breach must cause harm

(a)   The breach must cause harm of a kind which the court would compensate and which it was 'reasonable to foresee'.

(b)   Would the harm have happened anyway?

As Tingle (2002c) notes, reasonableness is a key concept in the law of negligence. The issue before the courts is not what a particular individual is expected to do in the circumstances, but instead what a 'reasonable person' would be expected to do (Carson 1996; Giliker and Beckwith 2000). Another issue is the problem which courts and investigators face with the 'hindsight fallacy'. As Macdonald and Macdonald (1999) point out, a bad outcome is in and of itself not evidence that a decision is mistaken; the fallacy of hindsight is to assume that it was. These authors criticise various official reports for this fallacy. They cite Carson (1996, p.10) to the effect that the court has to avoid hindsight, so why not help it?

Carson suggests that if the worker has a reason to believe that an event is possible but unlikely, then he or she should explicitly record that likelihood: 'Unless it can be shown that your estimate was inappropriate it will prove powerful in discouraging any court that the harm, which has now occurred, was more likely than it then seemed' (Carson 1996. p.10). He points out that workers can takes steps themselves to help the court and to jusitfy their decision making. However he also rightly argues that social service and social work managers have responsibilities too. Managers in the future may well find themselves, according to Carson, risking legal liability by not recognising that risk taking is a skill which deserves to be developed. Their responsibilities include ensuring that their staff are trained in risk assessment and the making of justifiable decisions.

Risk taking and restraint

The issue of restraint in heath and social care settings has received surprisingly little systematic attention either within the research literature or within the official literature produced by governmental bodies. Reviews of the literature in respect of children can be found in Selekman and Snyder (1997) and Mohr and Anderson (2001) and for adults in Evans and Strumpf (1989); Fisher (1994); and Mohr, Petti and Mohr (2003). Practical guidance can be found in Harris *et al.* (1996); Centre for Residential Child Care (1995); Mental Welfare Commission for Scotland (1998); see also Harris *et al.* 1996 on challenging behaviour.

The practice of restraint is widespread across the board for vulnerable children and vulnerable adults, yet its basis in legislation, codes of practice and other guidance is highly questionable. In Scotland, an attempt is being made to include the issue of restraint as part of the new national care standards that are being set for vulnerable children and adults (see e.g. Scottish Executive 2004b; 2004c; 2004d). For example, care homes are being encouraged to have written policies and procedures on restraint and to have staff trained and supported in the use of restraint.

Restraint takes many forms in the context of health and social care. It may be defined as:

> Restriction of the capacity of an individual to exercise freedom of movement or to take part in social interaction or other daily activities. In certain circumstances, this includes time-limited and specific action to prevent a person harming him/herself or other people.

This definition covers physical, chemical and electronic forms of restriction such as the use of drugs, restraints and electronic tagging. It allows for the inclusion of financial restrictions, such as in the case of guardianship or use of powers of attorney. It also means that lack of explicit policies and procedures relating to risk taking could be included, as this constitutes restraint, albeit in an indirect form. The importance of such policies is discussed in Chapter 4.

The definition indicates that the use of restraint should be specific and time-limited; its use should be clearly spelled out in policies that managers, staff, users and informal carers can easily access and understand. As far as possible, care should be 'restraint free' (Dunbar 1997; Reith and Bennett 1998). Inevitably, dilemmas will arise as to when restraint should and should not be used. Dealing with these dilemmas is part and parcel of the craft of the health and welfare professional and this is considered in greater detail in the next chapter.

Restraint and the law

The foregoing discussion suggests that a topic that deserves further attention is the legal basis for restraining vulnerable individuals in the context of health and social care. Given the importance of the topic, there is little in the way of coherent guidance within a framework that would win the approval of government, watchdog bodies and groups campaigning for the rights of vulnerable persons. This is in part a reflection of the 'hotchpotch' of legislative measures governing vulnerable people described above. What is required is a wide-ranging review of restraint in all its diverse forms – physical, chemical and electronic (e.g. through tagging) – in the context of human rights legislation and in the context of risk-taking approaches.

The Parliamentary Health Committee on Elder Abuse made recommendations on the use of restraint, including medication, and declared that 'actual physical restraint of older people, for example by the use of furniture, physical confinement, or electronic tagging, is obviously also completely unacceptable' (House of Commons Health Committee 2004, Recommendation 70).

In its evidence to the inquiry on elder abuse, the Government trod a more cautious and pragmatic line, indicated by the following quotation:

> The Government is clear that routine use of restraints and electronic tagging is not acceptable. However, occasionally on a case-by-case basis, their use may be justified... However, their use is no substitute for good care and care management, and must not be used to reduce care levels or control people's behaviour. (Department of Health 2003, para. 46)

The Committee asked the Commission on Social Care Inspection to publish findings in relation to physical restraint, e.g. in relation to care homes. In Northern Ireland, the Registration and Inspection Advisory Committee is reviewing the Guidelines on Use of Restraint in Residential and Nursing Homes, looking at a wider context, including human rights law.

There are no statutory provisions that govern the specific issue of restraint of vulnerable people in the UK. However, certain Acts can be interpreted to provide some guidance under UK law. In England and Wales, provisions are available under Acts like the National Assistance Act 1948 and Mental Health Act 1983; some regulations are provided which include more explicit guidelines on the use of physical restraint, such as the Domiciliary Care Agencies Regulations 2001. As noted earlier, there are moves to reform mental health law and the new Mental Health Bill has been the subject of critical debate, particularly by professionals who will have to try to work with any new provisions relating to restraint, detention and compulsory treatment.

In Scotland, the new mental health Act, Mental Health (Care and Treatment) (Scotland) Act 2003 represents the outcome of deliberations on restriction and detainment of people with mental disorders. There are similar powers to those provided in the current Act. These include emergency detention for up to 72 hours and short-term detention for up to 28 days. A Compulsory Treatment Order is available but must first be approved by a Tribunal; similar Tribunal powers are being advocated for England and Wales. However, there is still a mix of other measures that can be used for restraint; these include: Guardianship; Community Care Orders; the National Assistance Act 1948 (Section 47); and Tutor-Dative, which is an old provision that has recently been revived.

Throughout the UK, Common Law principles give a private individual the power lawfully to detain, in a situation of necessity, a person of unsound mind who is a danger to himself or others. Common law gives certain responsibilities to those who care for others in health and social care, the duty to care for and ensure the safety of those in their charge, and the right to restrain to prevent harm, as long as the restraint used is the minimum necessary.

This is currently the range of legal provisions that could be used to restrict or restrain vulnerable persons, such as those with mental disorder. However, the definition of restraint is important, as has been suggested above, and other statutory measures may be relevant. For example, if the meaning were broadened to include restraint of financial management, then provisions such as Curator Bonis, Enduring Powers of Attorney and certification of incapacity of patients in hospital could be included for consideration (Mental Welfare Commission for Scotland 1998); the Mental Capacity Bill brings in a new provision for Lasting Power of Attorney for England and Wales.

Towards a legal framework

Can a legal framework for taking risks in social care be developed? The question is worth turning on its head for a moment to consider the opposite issue: what basis is there for preventing people from taking risks or for restraining them in some way? There are five elements to be considered when thinking about this question, according to a Counsel and Care report (1992):

1. The area of *voluntarily accepted restrictions* – does the fact that a vulnerable adult, such as an older person, enters a care home also imply consent to any restraint? There is no basis in law to suggest that power over one's life is relinquished on entry.

2. The possibility of *legal action* – e.g. if something goes wrong any action to restrain must be justified in law or legal action may result.

3. The issue of *consent* is important, especially the issue of informed consent. This question must be put: is it possible to restrain another person lawfully and justifiably?

4. The matter of *legislation* – e.g. the use of 1948 National Assistance Act and its shortcomings; is there scope for progressive development and amendment of the law and Codes of Practice, such as current and proposed mental health legislation for older people who are mentally frail? (See the section above.)

5. The question of when *force* is justifiable – without consent, restraint is only lawful where a crime or breach of the peace is committed or in self-defence.

There are of course differences between preventing someone from taking a risk and actively restraining someone but the line between them can often be indistinct and unclear in practice. In keeping with the risk-taking model we are trying to promote we have to be prepared to justify our actions, to move away from unnecessary restraints and limitations and to increase choice in the lives of vulnerable people. By promoting a more positive conception of risk taking we can assist in the development of a framework to underpin the rights of the latter.

Rights

At the heart of many of the issues we have been considering in relation to risk taking lies the issue of rights. Should these form the framework for risk taking to work successfully? There are some difficult issues to consider here. These three questions are based on a discussion by Counsel and Care 1992:

1.   Should there be a right to take a risk?

2.   Should there be a *legal* right to comprehensive care and protection?

3.   Can compulsory intervention both respect dignity and be the minimum necessary to provide sufficient protection?

Another key question to consider is whether the law is an appropriate mechanism for ensuring rights in relation to risk taking.

These questions generated much lively discussion among the participants in the training courses run by the author, and much attention tends to be focused on the first question. Most participants felt that there should be a right to take a risk but wanted to see a recognition of the importance of *responsibilities.*

Any risk should be conditional on three things:

The competence of the individual

Rights of users ————————————— Responsibilities of staff

What If They Hurt Themselves? (Counsel and Care 1992) noted the different rights of residents (e.g. to self-determination); of carers and relatives (e.g. the right to see loved ones responsibly cared for); of service providers (e.g. the right to support when criticised) and of neighbours (e.g. some right to privacy and space of their own). None of these rights is unqualified. Many rights, if guaranteed unconditionally, would infringe the rights of others equally legitimately claimed. 'Rights need to be balanced against equivalent responsibilities', as the authors of the Counsel and Care report argue (1992, p.12).

However, participants in the training courses felt strongly that the equation had to work both ways. Both users and staff have responsibilities and rights. The mutual recognition of rights and responsibilities is important:

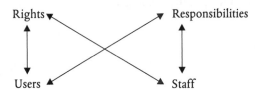

One group argued that clear, agreed policies and supervision were required, with clear lines of responsibility. Staff ought to participate in policy making and decision making. The group qualified their answer to question 2 with 'yes but', subject to availability, and queried the terms comprehensive, care and protection, expressing concern about 'who shouts loudest gets most' – would legal rights give them more clout? Professional judgements are important – not legal wrangles. For question 3, actions should be justifiable; again we need to define 'minimum' and 'sufficient protection'. Any intervention should be planned and multi-disciplinary in nature.

Just as rights are characteristically claimed by people for themselves, so responsibilities are most often allocated to others. Rights need to be balanced against responsibilities but in practice there will often be an ambiguous balance between the two. How practitioners can strike this balance is a crucial question for them to address.

The foregoing discussion indicates that welfare professionals need to be prepared to think through their risk decision making and to ensure that their decisions are justified. They should be able to demonstrate how and why their decisions were reached.

Conclusion

In this chapter, an attempt has been made to examine the context provided by the law as it presently stands in relation to risk taking and to speculate a little on what the future might hold. It has been argued that law can be a positive force, which welfare professionals would do well to study and to use, and that fears of litigation need to be addressed through training and education about the law and good practice. The vexed issue of rights and responsibilities of vulnerable people, carers and society and how these might be balanced in a progressive manner was also reviewed. In the chapter that follows, the notion of 'welfare dilemmas' and how they impact on professional practice is explored.

Chapter 3

Exploring Welfare Dilemmas

Introduction

In the course of their work, welfare professionals such as social workers, district nurses, hospital nurses and health visitors face important decisions concerning the welfare of their patients and clients. Family and other informal carers too are faced with difficult issues arising from the care of their relatives. Vulnerable people themselves often face hard choices with respect to their welfare options. In this chapter the important concept of the 'welfare dilemma' will be explored. It will be argued that this lies at the heart of professional practice and that, far from shying away, welfare professionals should embrace such dilemmas and explore creative and imaginative practice.

The notion of 'risk taking' raised in the first chapter will also be considered further. Emphasis will be placed on the significance of choice in the lives of vulnerable individuals. We will also look at issues for risk and safety; a case study to provide an example of a welfare dilemma and how it may be conceived and finally some examples of good practice in risk taking. A preliminary discussion of risk assessment will focus on the weighing up of risks for vulnerable people and their carers.

Welfare professionals and welfare dilemmas

How do social workers and other practitioners weigh up the often difficult decisions that they face and make tricky judgement calls? What factors are important in this process? Just how do professionals resolve the dilemmas they are so often faced with in their work? Some clarity in the key terms is required in order to give these questions due consideration.

For Congress (2000), recognising 'ethical dilemmas' that crop up in professional practice is crucial for practitioners, educators and students alike. The author however complains that that the literature on social work ethics, while growing, remains limited. According to Reamer (1983), the ethical dilemmas that social workers come across in practice can be put into three broad categories: direct service to individuals and families, design and implementation of social welfare policy and programmes, and relationships among professional colleagues. Risk-related work and decision making tend to cover all three of Reamer's categories.

To the extent that it is discussed, the focus of the literature tends to be on the 'professional dilemma', as in, for example, the work of writers such as Carson and Pritchard. Riley has defined a 'professional dilemma' as 'a situation in which a person who has specialist knowledge is confronted by choices between equally unacceptable alternatives' (Riley 1989, cited in Pritchard 1995). Dilemmas are about 'doing and sometimes about not doing'. The problem with this definition is that this entails not just professionals but other people too.

The term 'welfare dilemma' is preferred here, and it represents the starting point for answering the questions set out above. Further to Riley's definition, a welfare dilemma in terms of risk work can be defined as follows.

> A welfare dilemma involves choices that welfare professionals, vulnerable people, their informal carers and their communities face between options that entail possible benefits and possible harms. These choices may be equally acceptable but their outcomes essentially remain unknown.

There is no such thing as a 'risk free' option: all options hold potential risks. The choice between keeping someone apparently safe in a sheltered setting and in an unsheltered or open setting involves a consideration of the different types of risk which may arise in each option. Welfare dilemmas, when encountered by the practitioner, should not be ducked: they should be celebrated, as they provide the food and drink of professional's craft. Professional expertise needs to be addressed to help practitioners make judgement calls in the face of such dilemmas.

In his text on making decisions in social work, O'Sullivan defines decision making as 'the process of *making* a choice where the emphasis is on making, that is constructing, a choice' (1999, p.10). It occurs where there is a degree of recognition of a need or desire to make a choice. Decisions are based on 'expertise built up through experience'; they should not therefore be confused with simple reactions which are not thought through. There are two elements of note here: the first is the clear emphasis the author gives to choice, and the construction of the latter. The second is the highlighting of deliberation based on the social worker's own skills developed through his or her experiences. Both of these elements chime neatly with the themes of this book on risk taking. O'Sullivan does not define what he means by 'dilemma'. However, he does argue that an important part of 'sound decision making' should be a careful and systematic consideration of each option. Decision makers should be 'critically aware of the various influences on making a choice and clear about what they are basing their choice on' (1999, p.152).

The literature on decision making is rather less replete with studies of risk and decision making than one might have expected, given its importance in professional theory and practice. One recent study has been undertaken by Alaszewski *et al.* (1998) who looked at social workers, learning disability nurses, and district nurses visiting clients in their own homes for assessment and/or provision of services. They found mixed views of risk and on choice. Clients and their families faced the central focus of decisions and practitioners justified their decisions in terms of the consequences for the welfare of their client. Decisions became difficult when there were conflicts in the process, especially over perceptions by participants in the decision-making process. Alaszewski *et al.* also found little evidence that participants had been trained in formal decision-making processes or used structured decision-making processes.

Langan writes that 'mental health professionals commonly operate in conditions of uncertainty where risks are unclear and ethical dilemmas are rife' (1999, pp.154–155). Social workers lack clarity in assessing risk (Fisher *et al.* 1984; Sheppard 1990) yet definitions of risk are left to professional judgement. Professionals are given little guidance (Langan 1991), though there is more where there are more extreme risks. The prevailing emphasis on risk allows blame to be allocated when things go wrong (Douglas 1992). There is a widespread perception that community care is failing, that professionals are failing in their duty and that the public are at risk form those defined as having mental illness.

This in turn increases the likelihood of 'defensive practice', a finding previously noted by Fisher *et al.* 1984. Other authors have pointed to the need to resist defensive practice, for example in offender services (Kemshall 1996; Beaumont 1999) and in other areas of work (Carson 1995, 1996; Counsel and Care 1992; Pritchard 1997). More recently, there have been some studies of the knowledge and understanding of professionals, including studies of the rationales provided for risk assessments by social workers (Benbenishty, Osmo and Gold 2003) and the understanding by mental health workers of risk assessment (Gale *et al.* 2002; Gale, Hawley and Sivakumaran 2003). Further studies of the knowledge base of welfare professionals and their decision-making skills would, nonetheless, be a welcome addition to this literature.

Risk taking, welfare dilemmas and key tensions

While the literature has witnessed much recent discussion about definitions and perceptions of risk, comparatively little attention has been paid to the concept of 'risk taking', which is treated as a relatively unproblematic term. Alaszewski *et al.* suggest risk taking is 'concerned primarily with individual decisions about risk' (1998, p.17); this is contrasted with risk management, which is concerned with collective or group decisions. However, this is a less than clear distinction. Both risk taking and risk management can have individual or collective foci; the distinction lies in risk management being a process for monitoring and reviewing risk activities and decisions.

It is more useful to talk of risk taking as a general notion, of which risk assessment and risk management form particular activities and processes within the framework. Hence the emphasis is here on the risk-taking model of risk assessment. Risk taking will be defined here as undertaking a course of purposive action which may result in beneficial or harmful outcomes for the individual, as well as for others. It is these that help create welfare dilemmas for professionals, individuals and their families and friends.

In some instances cognisance can be taken of the law and guidance provided to support the courts and welfare agencies, e.g. in judging issues arising from the implications of mental incapacity. Stevenson (1999a) refers to the findings of the Law Commission (1995) which borrowed the term 'significant harm' from the Children Act 1989 (and the Children Scotland Act 1995), as the criterion for deciding on unacceptable risk (see the discussion in Appendix 1). This focuses the analysis on consideration of the damage which the risk has caused or may cause. Stevenson argues that 'the leanings of individual practitioners towards protection or autonomy' influence how they interpret phrases such as the risk of significant harm (1999a, p.213; see also Ayres' (1998) discussion of the latter).

The assessment of risk may not be in itself difficult, Stevenson argues, 'rather it is the decision to intervene to protect which may pose painful dilemmas' (1999a, p.202). In the case of older people, this often turns on the issue of mental capacity. 'Since life is inherently risky, assessment must focus upon the notion of unacceptable risk,' though she recognises that this will be subject to social definition in different times and cultures. Hence the assessment of risk should be this: 'Is the person exposed to, or likely to be exposed to, risk of significant harm?' (1999a, p.212) Thus, the primary objective is to minimise risk of significant harm.

Stevenson has usefully reviewed risks for older people, particularly in relation to abuse. There are a number of difficulties with her arguments. One is that the objective of the minimisation of significant harm, while laudable in itself, is a necessary but insufficient condition for promoting the quality of life of vulnerable people, including older persons. As has been argued elsewhere in this book, there is a need to look at the maximisation of opportunities for vulnerable people, facilitating their choices in respect of taking risks. Another problem is that if assessments just focus on 'unacceptable risk', there is a danger of ignoring assessing for positive risks.

Stevenson rightly argues that: 'it seems very important that the interaction of need with risk be at the heart of the process. In this way, the implications of the assessment, including the elements of risk, will be considered creatively, with a search for imaginative solutions to the tensions between autonomy and protection' (1999a, p.214). This is indeed an important argument: risk and need have to be taken together. There is a compelling argument that risk taking is in fact a need in itself, and therefore should form an essential component of the needs assessments of vulnerable individuals.

Parsloe (1999b) argues that understandings change over time. Staff have to learn to live with uncertainty. Their professional judgements, however, may not accord with the views of the person being assessed; and users and carers may well differ on the value of positive risk. In the view of some writers it will always be about walking a tightrope (Waterson 1999, p.278; Connelly 2002, p.125).

The borderline between 'acceptable and 'unacceptable' risk has proved a rather elusive boundary in terms of definition and delimitation by writers in this area. The notion of an 'unacceptable risk' is a popular one with some welfare professionals and it has received some treatment in the literature. (The work of Olive Stevenson has already been cited above.) There is, however, a need to be wary about how such notions are used and the assumptions which are made. As Stevenson acknowledges, what constitutes unacceptable risk may vary over time and between cultures. A key difficulty remains the need not to lose sight of acceptable or more positive risks, and how these might be enhanced, not just how the risk of 'significant harm' can be reduced.

Some pointers can be discerned in debates over the protection of vulnerable adults. Brown (2002) writes about the 'protection agenda' and helpfully reviews some of the issues associated with concerns to protect 'vulnerable adults' from violence, abuse or exploitation, and the search for safeguards. She rightly talks of tension between empowering people who are not traditionally powerful and introducing checks and balances which limit the influence of groups who have and (ab)use power over them. She notes that the agenda is now moving towards concerns about the equal protection of vulnerable people, not just about existing safeguards. This is true but only to an extent: the agenda, partly fuelled by media-driven concerns, is still rather confused, dominated by a concern with checks and balances, rather than developing the implications of the empowerment approach. This concern is reflected in developing policy and practice in Scotland, where a law, the Adults With Incapacity Act (Scotland) 2000, has been passed to protect vulnerable persons from abuse, and in England where the Mental Capacity Bill is before Parliament.

For Preston-Shoot (2001), a clear tension still exists between protection and self-determination, paternalism and autonomy. These tensions, we can add, are to be found in current policies concerning vulnerable adults, a point which will be returned to later. Preston-Shoot is wary of the argument made by writers such as Pritchard (1995) that social workers cannot impose solutions: they can only offer support and explain options. This writer criticises Pritchard for the assumption that victims can exercise control over decision making and proposes that there is need to consider the importance of values.

Balancing acts: harm and safety

In everyday life many actions have elements of danger. However, some dangers are more in the eye of the observer than in the mind of the participant. Voluntary risk taking can only occur when the risks have been identified, enabling individuals to make personal choices about types and levels of risk which are appropriate in certain situations. As Stevenson writes, 'since risk is part of life, how do we draw a line between "acceptable" and "unacceptable"?' (1999a, p.201).

To help answer such questions, we need to set about unpacking the concept of 'risk taking' further, including the notion of 'voluntary risk taking'. This involves the idea of opting to take risks willingly. Following the Centre for Policy on Ageing report *Living Dangerously* (Wynne-Harley 1991), the idea of voluntary risk taking can usefully be broken down as follows.

Individual choice and setting limits

The setting of *personal* limits is the key to risk taking. Two aspects of risk taking need to be distinguished:

- practical – 'taking chances', e.g. running for a bus, using unsuitable equipment or standing on a chair
- recreational – 'getting a buzz', e.g. activities which stimulate and offer excitement.

The relative importance of each of these categories may influence the setting of personal limits.

Calculations and trade-offs

Restrictions and personal limits may be seen as ways of protecting independence and quality of life; in other situations the idea of perceived risk is an important ingredient in a stimulating and satisfying life. The major factor influencing attitudes to risk, according to Wynne-Harley (1991), is the maintenance of independence and autonomy.

Assumptions about normality, for example, in old age

The use of stereotypes about old age and our 'ageist' attitudes prevent us from seeing that older age is characterised by great diversity of ability and lifestyle. Many older people themselves have low expectations about what they can do and what they can achieve. They share the prevalent negative attitudes towards old age, no longer seeing themselves as part of mainstream society. As Wynne-Harley writes: 'In doing so, they may accept the rights of those who are younger to make decisions for them, to reduce their autonomy, to eliminate choice and risk from their lives' (1991, p.27).

Importance of rights

The importance of the rights of older persons in relation to risk and choice is also highlighted by Wynne-Harley: 'Reasonable, informed and calculated risk taking plays an important part in contributing to the quality of life for young and old; this is a matter of choice, demonstrating an individual's right of self-determination and autonomy' (1991, p.29).

To illustrate some of the welfare dilemmas which can arise we shall examine a fictitious case study of an older woman.

Case study: Senga Craigie

This case study, adapted from Norman (1988), is set in an urban environment, with potential hazards for those living close by.

Senga Craigie is 78 and lives on the ground floor of a block of council flats in the city of Glasgow. She is a widow with one daughter, Isobel, who lives a complicated bus journey away. The daughter is the breadwinner for her own household and has a husband who is long-term sick and unemployed. Her only child has left home, so she has a spare room. Senga is suffering from a longstanding and increasingly severe dementia with consequent serious neglect of herself and her flat and some nuisance to her neighbours. She is reluctant to accept the help of anyone except her daughter and will not eat meals-on-wheels though she seems to keep quite healthy on a diet of bread, cheese and tea. A small fire which was caused by airing her clothes too close to the heater has brought the neighbours up in arms saying 'something must be done!' Senga is fiercely independent and does not want to leave her home but she retains a deep respect for the authority of officialdom and would not actively resist being moved.

Questions

1. What are the choices facing Senga and her daughter Isobel?

2. What are the dangers and what are the advantages of each choice for Senga, for Isobel and for the social services?

Suggested approach for tackling this case study

CHOICE NO. 1: STAYING AT HOME

Danger to Mrs Craigie

- Painful death by fire or accident
- Slow death by malnutrition and neglect
- Increasing mental isolation and bewilderment at inability to understand and control environment
- Development of paranoid fears
- Antagonism from neighbours

Advantages to Mrs Craigie

- No traumatic change
- Stays in a familiar place
- Minimal loss of identity
- Wishes respected

Danger to daughter

- Guilt
- Increased strain and cost from travelling to give care in a deteriorating situation
- Repercussions of this on the family
- Possible blame from family members for not taking mother to live with her

Advantages to daughter

- Does not have to share her home
- May transfer guilt by blaming social services for the decision
- Can still give help – as opposed to an institutional situation

Danger to social services

- Extensive domiciliary services will be needed
- Pressure from neighbours, GP, etc.
- Possible fire or accident with resultant bad publicity

Advantages to social services

- Respects self-determination and independence
- Other solutions possible later
- Residential care place available for another client

CHOICE NO. 2: MOVING HOME

Danger to Mrs Craigie

- Anger at forced move
- Disorientation
- Loss of independence and self-care
- Possible antagonism from family members

Advantages to Mrs Craigie

- Increased physical safety
- More social contact
- Better diet, warmth, etc.

Danger to daughter and family

- Lost earning power
- Lost privacy and freedom
- Marital relationships might suffer
- Potentially very long-term responsibility of increasing severity of mother's disability

Advantages to daughter and family

- Relief from guilt and anxiety
- Less travelling

Danger to social services

- Possibility of breakdown in daughter's care, with institutional care then the only solution left
- Cost of giving the daughter appropriate support

Advantages to social services

- Socially acceptable, cheap solution (at least in the short term)

CHOICE NO. 3: MOVING TO RESIDENTIAL CARE

Danger to Mrs Craigie

- Anger
- Disorientation
- Loss of self-care skills
- Reduced family contact
- Possible antagonism from residents

Advantages to Mrs Craigie

- Safety
- Social contact (if it is a good home)
- Warmth and diet
- Not being a burden
- No conflict with family/neighbours

Danger to daughter

- Guilt
- Resulting family conflict
- Little opportunity to give personal care
- Possible dissatisfaction with home

Advantages to daughter

- Home and lifestyle unchanged
- No anxiety about safety

Danger to social services

- Residential care place used up
- Self-determination not respected
- Home may be reluctant to go on coping

Advantages to social services

- Safety
- Flat freed
- Resources not used on domiciliary care
- Neighbours happy

The key to tackling this case study is to understand the need to set out the choices facing Senga and her daughter and assess the advantages and disadvantages accordingly. (For simplicity's sake, these choices have been here narrowed to three, but more are available, e.g. sheltered housing, very sheltered support at home and so on.) At the heart of this lies negotiation. The development of a shared negotiated responsibility for risk taking is essential; however, as Gilmour, Gibson and Campbell (2003) note, it requires resources and support to enable professionals, families and persons with dementia to do this.

What does this case study and those in the appendix show? First, they illustrate the importance of the making of choices and the examination of options. There are acute dilemmas here that were tackled by the training participants. Second, they show the importance of compromise and negotiation among those affected by the risk decision, including Senga and her daughter Isobel, the neighbours and health and welfare professionals. This points up the importance of these as key skills for professionals to develop and refine. Third, they demonstrate how important it is to weigh up the advantages and disadvantages, the pros and cons, of each option. This is a basic requirement of risk assessment. The next chapter develops this point, suggests ways for refining our approach to risk assessment and considers key steps necessary for this process.

Good practice and risk taking

There has been a growth of interest in 'good practice' and 'best practice' in health and welfare settings in relation to risk (see for example Kemshall and Pritchard 1996, 1997; Regester and Larkin 2002), though definitions of laudable practice remain rather diffuse. Let us now consider some examples of interesting practice with respect to risk taking, as well as the use of restraint.

V Ward, Seacroft Hospital in Leeds

The philosophy of the nurses running this ward has been mentioned in Chapter 1. This is an assessment unit with 26 beds for people with dementia, many of whom find difficulty in orientating themselves, and has these features:

- explicit approach to risk taking – ward philosophy is spelled out
- senior staff with the attitude that 'it's OK to get things wrong'
- education is seen as essential – for both nurses and relatives
- open door policy in afternoons
- unescorted visits by patients to hospital shop
- positioning of furniture to allow free movement in ward.

(Personal communication, Seacroft Hospital
Nursing Development Unit)

Bole Hill View, Sheffield

This is a local authority home with 25 long-stay beds and with these features:

- a distinct philosophy – individualised care, not confrontation, and 'resident oriented, not task oriented'
- policy of 'calculated risk management', e.g. open door policy
- senior staff support care workers
- communication – regular meetings between staff and with carers too.

(Norman (1987))

Summary of 14 case studies

In a study of 14 specialist care units for people with dementia, Norman (1987) found features relevant to the provision of good care, including the ability to exercise choice and self-determination in daily living. The following features were identified, although they varied from unit to unit:

- no use of geriatric chairs
- minimal use of day-time sedation
- activities outside the home given equal importance to those inside the home
- provision of good quality and dignified personal clothing
- relaxed and flexible regimes for getting up and going to bed
- dressing process in private

However, most staff in these units 'took it for granted that their responsibility to protect from physical harm outweighed residents' rights to freedom to come and go at will' (1987, p.66).

'The Risk Factor'

The magazine *Community Care* has an occasional feature entitled 'The Risk Factor'. This useful series provides case studies of social workers and other staff faced with difficult risk decisions and includes brief case notes, arguments for and against risk, and independent comment. It includes accounts of dilemmas for workers dealing with issues such as independent living, mental illness, learning disability, drug misuse and so on (Bond 1998; George 1997a, 1997b, 1998a, 1998b; Hopkins 2003, 2004a, 2004b, 2004d). How far each particular case constitutes 'good practice' is a matter for debate but they highlight a number of interesting issues for social care professionals.

Reviewing a sample of 'The Risk Factor' articles suggests the following features:

- clear recognition of a welfare dilemma
- careful evaluation of arguments for and against taking the risk
- honest assessment of potential problems
- close working with other agencies
- engagement with client

- follow-up of client outcome – how the person is coping after taking the risk
- capacity for reflection.

The case studies show the importance of the practitioner(s) thinking through the dilemma and weighing up the evidence. One limitation is the lack of information about longer-term outcome, e.g. a report six months to a year after the risk has been taken, to see how the client is getting on (though a follow-up of one of the more controversial case studies has been promised; see Hopkins 2004c). The lack of inclusion of case studies of risk taking that have had adverse outcomes is also a limitation in terms of learning. Finally, the absence of independent validation of the case study limits its applicability. Nonetheless, this series has been a very useful one and managers and practitioners interested in risk taking would do well to examine these case studies.

Conclusion

The above examples show that the area of risk taking is still very much under development but that there are health and social care professionals prepared to try a new approach towards improving the quality of life of vulnerable people. This chapter has emphasised the centrality of the 'welfare dilemma' in risk taking, the importance of the facilitation of choices in the lives of vulnerable individuals and their informal carers, and some preliminary steps towards weighing the risks involved for the individuals and their carers. In the next few chapters, the discussion moves on to examine a more systematic approach to help guide risk decisions.

Chapter 4

Principles, Policies and Models

Introduction

Having set out the key context for considering risks for vulnerable people, the discussion can now turn to outlining a systematic approach to risk taking and introducing the Person-centred Risk Assessment and Management System (PRAMS) model. This chapter is largely concerned with describing and explaining the importance of developing principles and policies for risk taking; these form the first two stages of the PRAMS model. This provides an essential framework for risk decisions. Brearley rightly made this seminal point in his discussion of risk: 'The argument for an organised and systematic approach to the understanding of risk is of central importance in social work' (1982, p.156).

As part of a systematic approach, key values, principles and policies need to be addressed and spelled out. In the literature there has been a greater recognition of the importance of risk policies; general discussions of the topic can be found in Alaszewski *et al.* (1998), for example. However there have as yet been few examples of effective risk policies and core guidance for welfare agencies, managers and practitioners to follow. In this chapter an attempt is made to make good this deficit within the literature.

PRAMS: A systematic approach to risk taking

What is needed is a systematic approach for the assessing and managing of risks with which care professionals and other staff, vulnerable individuals and their families can work. PRAMS (Person-centred Risk Assessment and

Management System) is one such approach. PRAMS involves work on these main elements, which are discussed below:

- establishing principles
- creating policies
- assessing risk
- devising risk plans
- managing risk.

PRAMS is a systematic approach developed by the author for the assessment and management of risk in community and longstay settings. It provides a comprehensive yet flexible framework for promoting good practice in risk taking in the field of welfare with which care professionals and other staff, vulnerable individuals and their families can work. It is based on research and training exercises with a range of welfare professionals from different disciplines in social work, health care and housing, and embodies an explicit philosophy of risk taking which seeks to enhance the quality of life of individuals in need of support and to improve the quality of risk decisions made by practitioners. It is intended to cover all vulnerable persons, however severe their disability or illness.

PRAMS involves work on five distinct yet related stages. The first stage entails the establishing of principles; here staff are encouraged to discuss and agree key statements intended to guide the assessment and management process and its intended outcomes. In the next stage, issues for developing risk policies in the workplace are examined and the rationale, function and content of these policies are discussed. The third stage involves staff considering different assessment models, as well as the key steps for the identification and assessment of risk. Staff can work on specially constructed vignettes, case studies and scenarios designed to explore dilemmas and develop skills for making decisions. In the following stage, the notion of 'risk planning' is introduced and staff devise planned responses to assessments. The fifth stage deals with models of risk management and the key steps for managing risks; here again staff can be set to work on cases designed to test decision making skills.

PRAMS is designed to be an interlinked system; practitioners are encouraged to consider the connections between the stages and continually to review what they have learned. Another key theme is that of developing skills: each stage entails work on particular skills. To take an example, the art of making 'judgement calls' is further explored at the assessment stage (see Chapter 5 and Chapter 8).

Stage 1: Setting out key principles

The initial phase of PRAMS involves considering, agreeing and setting out the underlying principles that are required to guide managers, practitioners, users and informal carers in risk taking. The examples of key principles outlined below have been derived from the results of training exercises with managers and frontline staff in multidisciplinary settings, as well as service users and informal carers. Participants were asked to outline a number of general principles to govern approaches to risk taking. They did this in small groups and the results were fed back to the main group. These were in turn used to build up guidance. Examples of guiding statements include:

Risk involves the following:

- it is an essential and unavoidable part of everyday life
- (therefore) risk taking is a *normal* part of everyday life
- it involves choice
- it can help promote the dignity and rights of the individual.

However, there also has to be an acknowledgement that *rights* will have to be balanced against *responsibilities*.

- risk taking involves *compromise* and *negotiation*.

In addition, we should be prepared to accept these statements:

- beware hasty assumptions about individual lifestyles
- the autonomy of the individual is paramount
- be prepared for a long process of discussion – *communication* is the key
- community expectations are particularly important and have to be taken into account.

Identifying good practice and bad practice

The authors of the Counsel and Care report (1992) have rightly stressed the links between good practice and recognition of the need to take risks. In the previous chapter, it was noted that there has been a growth of interest in good practice in risk taking in health and social care, but that definitions currently remain less than clear and precise. In the light of this, it is important that managers and practitioners are asked to think about their own understandings of what counts as good and bad practice and to try to secure a measure of consensus around definitions and understandings.

In the training exercises described above, participants were asked to identify and explore examples of good practice:

- why did it work?
- what were the key elements?

and bad practice:

- on what occasions did good practice fail?
- what were the reasons?

Examples are given in Tables 4.1 and 4.2. There was some reluctance to explore bad practice, perhaps because many participants came from small communities where everyone knew everyone else. Few examples were given but some helpful illustrations were provided. However, general principles for avoiding bad practice began to emerge and were built into the next exercise, identifying some key principles to underpin good practice in risk taking.

Developing guidance

Participants were asked to think about appropriate guidance on good practice risk taking, relevant to their own workplace and to the people they had to look after. They were first asked to discuss and agree a number of general principles to govern risk taking approaches and the promotion of good practice for their colleagues and clients. They did this in small groups and the results were fed back to the main group.

Specific examples were given and some of the particular issues associated with the example were explored in the small groups and in the feedback. The open door policy and more relaxed regime at a residential unit (Viewforth) provided a useful illustration for participants to consider.

Table 4.1 Key points for good practice

Reccommended practice	Staff to implement practice
Staff to be *enabled* through training and support • staff supervision • staff education and awareness	Scottish Executive/ Social Work Dept. (SWD) /Health Board managers (HB)
Guidelines for management of risk from employing authorities	SWD/HB
Management support to assist decision making	SWD/HB managers
Issues of clients' rights/choice/consultation have to be addressed	Everyone
The person's family has a right to be involved	Everyone
Public education and raising general awareness is important	Everyone
Staffing levels to be addressed, e.g. at night time	HB/SWD managers
Maintaining skills, e.g. self-medication	Managers/care staff
Good communications especially teamwork/support network	Teams
Individual goal planning, e.g. shopping/training	Teams/key workers
Right to *choice* and individual lifestyles	Everyone
Prior knowledge before admissions to care especially to determine acceptable risks	Care staff
Risks assessed for each individual within a clear framework	Care staff
Risk factors identified in environment and reduced to an acceptable level, e.g. risk audit	Care staff
Be prepared for negotiation/compromise/agreement among all parties	Everyone
Support of senior staff	Senior managers
Internal policy guidelines on restraint and risk taking	Managers
Information strategy is essential – need to give adequate information	Scottish Executive HB/SWD/occupational therapists/GPs etc.
Care plan should be clear and agreed – risks to be spelled out as far as possible in care plan and written down clearly in advance	Care staff
Regular reviews of practice at all levels for individual clients and staff ongoing to meet changing needs	Care managers/care staff
Professional decision making has to be developed and supported	Care staff, managers
Flexibility is important	Care staff

Table 4.2 Key points for bad practice

Practice to avoid	Staff to implement practice
Not listening to views of user	Everyone
Giving undue weight to views of relatives	Care staff
Putting someone at risk through carelessness or neglect	Care staff
Simply reacting to crisis without thinking through appropriate steps	Everyone
Inappropriate risk taking, e.g. frail elderly driving cars without due care or oversight	GPs/DVLC
Badly written guidance for residents and carers	HB/SWD Scottish Executive
Lack of adequate resources	Scottish Executive HB/SWD
Lack of training	Scottish Executive HB/SWD
Poor management	Scottish Executive SWD/HB Management committees
Lowering expectations of clients and collusion	Everyone
Removing a person's individuality, by taking away their rights of self-medication	Care staff
Unnecessary use of sedation and restraint, discussion needed on wandering	Care staff
Misuse of equipment, e.g. chairs or cot sides – importance of choice for residents	Care staff

- chair restraints
- feeding
- making people have baths
- witholding of information to prevent discrimination, e.g. asthma/epilepsy

Setting out risk policies

Risk taking works best where agencies and units (or wards) have an explicit risk policy. In the Introduction, it was noted that social services employers are being urged to develop and set out explicit policies on risk assessment (Scottish Social Services Council 2003). A clear policy provides a framework for good practice for the benefit of the individual, the family and the staff involved. It can help them, according to Lawson (1996):

- make sound risk decisions
- feel good about the decisions they have made
- fully understand and articulate why they have made specific decisions.

In addition, it will give staff support in making difficult risk decisions, assist in justifying those decisions and make for a more consistent service.

As Carson (n.d.) notes, good employers ought to develop risk-taking policies to help their staff make quality decisions, to help managers do their job better and to provide a philosophy to support professionals. He makes the important point that following a risk policy and procedure makes *legal liability* when harms occur less likely. Not to do so could mean a risk decision is taken *negligently*.

Furthermore, the authors of the Counsel and Care document on the use of restraint argue that:

> it must be a starting point of good practice to recognise need to take risks, to exercise good judgment in ensuring risks are responsibly taken and to create structures which facilitate a prudent assessment of the risks both before they are taken and without recrimination respectively. (1992, p.12)

The aim of a good risk policy is to provide the framework for these structures so that this approach can be implemented in practice.

Setting out a risk-taking policy

The first step is to set out and put in place a policy on risk. This is important as it is a written statement of the aims and values of your agency with respect to risk and describes the role that staff have. It deals with what the agency expect of its staff and what users and carers can expect of your agency. More detail on what risk policies do, why they are needed and the areas that should be covered by them, is provided below.

WHAT A POLICY ON RISK TAKING DOES

- It outlines the principles upon which risks are treated in your agency.
- It defines the roles, rights and responsibilities of staff and your agency.

- It includes a code of practice governing the conduct of staff within your agency.

WHY RISK POLICIES ARE NEEDED

- to outline to staff, carers and users of services how and why risk taking will be dealt with
- to prevent decisions being based on unwritten rules, prejudice, favouritism – or crucially, negligence
- to outline what is expected of staff
- to clarify what users have a right to expect from your agency
- to raise awareness among staff about risk and its management
- to clarify boundaries
- to provide a basis for regular monitoring and evaluation of risk taking practices.

CONTENTS OF POLICIES

A policy on risk taking may include statements on:

- definitions of what counts as 'risk'
- rights and responsibilities of staff
- rights and responsibilities of users
- reporting and recording procedures
- training of staff
- support for staff, including counselling
- grievance, disciplinary and complaints procedures
- health and safety
- monitoring and evaluation.

DEVELOPING AN EFFECTIVE POLICY

The aims of an effective policy for assessing and managing risk are, according to Littlechild (1996):

1.   To enable effective recognition of areas of risk for:

   - work setting
   - types of situations
   - client groups
   - individual responses.

2.   Where there is concern about aggression and violence, to reduce risk by:

   - agency
   - team
   - peer group
   - individual awareness.

3.   To reduce isolation of staff, physically and emotionally, by planning based on 1 and 2 and to increase collective support.

Where there are issues to do with challenging behaviour or the assessment and management of aggressive behaviour, then it is imperative that managers and staff develop an effective framework for risk policies and procedures (Titterton 1997).

Some examples of developing risk policies

It is useful to consider some working examples of agencies that have tried to develop risk policies. We consider some examples from the statutory and voluntary sector and look at some of the differences. All of these examples have undertaken training and attempted to develop the PRAMS approach for their own workplace, staff and clients.

   The Mungo Foundation (formerly the Archdiocese of Glasgow Community Social Services) has made great efforts to address the issues raised by risk and risk taking. The organisation provides care for an impressive range of groups: young parents, those affected by drugs and alcohol, mental health, dementia, and provides different forms of care including respite and shortstay projects, as well as longstay residential projects. A training programme based on PRAMS was initiated and followed up with training for project managers, as well as senior care staff. Lively discussion has been taking place within both the projects and the office about risk taking policy and guidelines, with the PRAMS model at its heart.

Sense Scotland is an agency which was established to help people with multiple disabilities, including people who are deaf and blind. Its workers face difficult situations in caring. Since the agency sent a member of staff on the PRAMS training course they have been attempting to develop a risk policy. Albyn Housing Association is in a similar position. Based in the north of Scotland, the agency provides a range of accommodation and care services for young people and those who are homeless. Albyn put all its staff through the course and has been developing policies and practice for more creative ways of working with vulnerable people.

Fife and East Renfrewshire are two social work departments that have emphasised the importance of training their staff, and following the impact of training they have both been actively involved in developing risk policies and in attempting to improve practice.

In Dumfries and Galloway, attempts have been made by community hospital staff, primary care staff and carers to forge a multiagency approach to defining risks and agreeing, influenced by the PRAMS model. Managers and staff are keen to develop a shared approach to tackling risks such those faced by older people coming out of hospital, and set days aside for training and for review of common issues in risk work.

Finally, in Shetland joint training was provided in Isleburgh Community Centre in Lerwick, with an interesting mix of participants from social work, health, housing and the independent sector. This led to a number of changes. Staff at Viewforth Hospital developed a policy and risk schedule and an open door regime; nurses in the dementia wards also attempted to develop a risk-taking approach. Staff in remote and rural locations especially need to develop a risk-taking approach, as they often have to make decisions on their own in risky situations.

Conclusion

In this chapter the importance of setting a systematic approach to risk taking has been argued and the PRAMS model outlined. The first two stages of this were presented: first, the setting out of key principles and second, the devising of risk policies. This provides an essential framework for supporting staff and vulnerable people. Finally, examples were considered of agencies that have been prepared to think through and develop their risk taking approach. Now we will look at the third stage of PRAMS, namely risk assessment.

Chapter 5

Risk Assessment

Introduction

Risk assessment is a topic which has grown massively in interest, reflected in both the academic and professional literatures, as will be seen below. The reasons behind this explosion of interest are generally the same as those behind the interest in risk discussed in earlier chapters. However, there are specific concerns about assessment, as evidenced in demands on welfare professionals from managers, as well as policy guidance at local and national levels. This emphasis on risk assessment is critically examined later in this chapter. First, though, the literature on the assessment of risk is reviewed, problems with this literature discussed and gaps identified. (The review does not assume there is a uniform body of literature on the topic: here it is quite legitimate to talk of *literatures*.) Second, a system for risk assessment that builds on the arguments of the preceding chapters is presented. A definition of risk assessment, along with its main principles and characteristics, is put forward, and key steps for assessing risk are outlined as a guide for welfare professionals as the third stage in the PRAMS approach.

The literature on risk assessment

The literature on risk assessment in health and social care has grown considerably of late. This is in response to the growth of 'risk' as a topic for reasons already discussed in Chapter 1, particularly the demands for clarification of the issues and the search for guidelines to assist decision making. Indeed an even larger literature might have been expected, given the current preoccupation with the subject, but it is clear that there are extensive gaps. In some fields, such as mental health, risk assessment has become a 'fashionable buzz phrase', as Gunn (1997, p.163) has said. This review was carried out using online databases such as BIDS, ASSIA, CINAHL and Medline (including the catalogue at the Health Scotland library) deploying key words such as risk assessment and risk taking, and builds on and updates a previous search undertaken by the author (Titterton 1999).

Some fields of studies, such as health promotion, have operated with risk assessment discourses across the wide range of topics the field covers, such as HIV and AIDS, young people, coronary heart disease, dietary problems and so on. There have been helpful critiques of this discourse but work is still required to think through the implications of the positive conception of risk taking argued for in this book. However, like social workers, health promotion specialists are increasingly facing risk taking in their work.

A major difficulty is apparent in examining this literature, particularly in the field of mental health. The emphasis remains on assessing for the risk of harmful or adverse outcomes (see, e.g. Robinson and Collins 1999). The concerns are with 'dangerousness' and risk in terms of violence to self or others (Howlett 1997; Monahan 1988; Potts 1995; Reed 1997; Skeem et al. 2004; Steadman et al. 1993). Langan (1999) states that in the 1990s there was a shift to more powers to control individuals seen as a risk to others. Citing also Kemshall et al. (1997), she argues that risk and danger have become the criteria for eligibility for services, rather than need. Mental health policy is in danger of being driven by these 'appalling but relatively rare tragedies' (1999, p.154). The little research that has been done on social workers in this area (e.g. Fisher et al. 1984; Sheppard 1990) reveals that they lack clarity in assessing risk, an argument that is extended to nursing staff as well (see e.g. CRAG/SCOTMEG Working Group on Mental Illness 19995).

While some approaches place emphasis on the professional or clinical judgement of the individual making the assessment, others emphasise the identification of factors that can be shown as statistically significant in predicting risk. However, professionals have also been shown consistently to be poor at predicting risk accurately; moreover, there is uncertainty as to how this accuracy can be bettered. This is compounded by differential perceptions of risk among professionals themselves. Gale *et al.* (2003) in their study of risk assessment by mental health workers claim that individuals perceive risk differently and that female assessors showed some tendency towards greater caution. They also point out that there is a 'surprising lack of good evidence to back current practice' (2003, p.81). In common with writers such as Smith (2001), they rightly draw attention to the need to work in partnership with other agencies and disciplines.

Some topics have received greater attention than others. It is not difficult to find discussions of suicide risk (Gunn 1997; Inskip, Harris and Barraclough 1998; Lyon 1997; Rossau and Mortensen 1997). There has of late been an increase in interest in assessing negative risks in relation to populations labelled as 'deviant'. These include: sexual offenders (Barker and Morgan 1993; Campbell 1995; Darjee 2003; McEwan and Sullivan 1996; O'Callaghan and Print 1994; Scottish Office 1997b); those who are or who have been involved in the criminal justice system and who may re-offend (Beaumont 1999; Horsefield 2003; Kemshall 1996, 2000; Petrunik 2002; Raynor *et al.* 2002; Roberts, Doren and Thornton 2002; Scottish Office 1998); drug misusers (Argall and Cowderoy 1997; Griffiths and Waterston 1996;); substance use (Stockwell and Toubourou 2004); and forensic mental health (Kelly, Simmons and Gregory 2002; Petrila 2004). The important, but relatively neglected, topic of self-harm in children and young people has also received some attention (Chitsabesan *et al.* 2003). There has been a recent growth of interest in risk assessment in relation to sex offenders and this is considered separately in Appendix I.

It is evident that the preoccupation with assessing negative risks such as potential harm or danger is particularly pronounced in respect of children (Berkowitz 1991; Bolen 2003; Corby 1996; Department of Health 1988, 2000, 2004a; English and Pecora 1994; Garrett 2003; Green and Mason 2002; Kinnair 2003; Scott 1998; Scottish Executive 2002, 2004b, 2004c; Scottish Office 1997a; Shlonsky and Gambrill 2001; Sinclair and Bullock 2002; Waterhouse and Carnie 1992). This is related to the negative construction of risk in studies of child welfare and child protection. Here risk assessment is focused on the prevention of abuse, especially of a sexual or physical nature (Bannister 1998; Barker and Araji 1998; Craissati 1998; DePaufils and Zwravin 2001). There has latterly been a broader debate about children and risk, including concerns about the 'overprotection of children' but this has largely involved criticism of parents, not professionals. A critique of risk assessment by professionals is overdue. There are nonetheless encouraging signs of a reconsideration of child abuse and child protection, particularly in Scotland, and this is also discussed separately in the first appendix.

The need for children to face risks as part of their development is insufficiently acknowledged in the literature. Writers like Parton, who elsewhere has recognised the ambiguity at the heart of risk work (1998), have so far not responded to this challenge (see for example Parton, Thorpe and Wattam 1997). Anglin (2002) has rightly argued for the need for transformation in respect to risk and child protection. While Houston and Griffiths (2000) call for a shift in paradigims concerning risk and child protection, to a subjectionist approach where contested meanings about risk become the focus for work, they unfortunately stop short of taking this developmental view of risk into their paradigm.

For Sargent, assessing risk is a 'mixture of art and science' (1999, p.184). She has provided a helpful overview of the main assessment models for children, raising concerns that current norms of assessment are still rooted in white, middle class, gendered ideology; cultural factors, such as ethnicity, are often overlooked. She also contends that child protection that is aimed at the detection and prevention of abuse and harm is looking through too narrow a window. The complexities of child and family relationships are ignored. This is a useful message which will be returned to later.

For adolescents, it is possible to detect a greater ambivalence about risk in relation to 'risk behaviours' (Maggs *et al.* 1997; Plant and Plant 1992). The idea that risk is exciting for young people is picked up by some of the literature. Health promotion has attempted to take account of this in some aspects of work. Nonetheless, there is also a sense that risk is something to be avoided, rather than something to be lived with and something which can provide beneficial learning opportunities. However, interesting insights have been provided by the work of Aggleton who, inspired by the notion of 'cultures of risk' linked to social and economic circumstances, has developed the notion of 'cultures of health' (Aggleton 1996; Dryfoos 1990; Health Education Authority (HEA) 1998; Petersen and Leffert 1995).

As the HEA notes, the value in this sort of approach is that it reminds us that 'many, if not most, young people engage in risky behaviour, but we know very little about how individuals move in and out of cultures of risk over time, and what determines the fact that some individuals are able to move on and some are not' (1998, p.13). Rightly, the HEA also calls for longitudinal studies of risk taking in children, young people and young adults to help gain this sort of knowledge. Moore and Parsons (2000) have outlined a research agenda for the examination of risk taking by adolescents.

The topic of coping provides a valuable research resource, one where the practical implications remain to be spelled out for both welfare planners and professionals (Titterton 1992). Coping and risk taking provides a fruitful research avenue to explore. Langan points out that: 'We have little or no research about the "protective factors" … in individuals' lives which serve to reduce risk whether that be to self or others' (1999, p.172).

There is a growing body of evidence relating to resilience and protective factors and their role in relation to emotional and mental health and well-being (Titterton, Hill and Smart 2002). A rich literature on children and young people and the role of risk and protective factors can be found (e.g. Anthony 1987; Rutter 1993; Sameroff 2001). In this body of work, there is much food for thought on the links between risk and resilience. The difficulty is that little attention has so far focused on risk mechanisms and processes, something which Rutter acknowledges. Moreover, here too risk is conceived in terms of adverse consequences. The potential of risk as a learning process for children and young people has not been exploited by researchers. The interconnections between risk, resilience and protective factors also require more detailed attention from the research community (see e.g. Titterton *et al.* 2002).

In the case of vulnerable adults, criticisms of the limited view of risk have already been advanced in Chapter 1. This is clearly reflected in risk assessment, where assessing for risk avoidance. The example of people with mental health problems has already been cited (see also Ryan 1996, 1997; Scott 1998). For people with learning disabilities, risk was evidently perceived in negative terms but more recently a growing literature of a more positive nature is to be found (Heyman 1998; Manthorpe *et al.* 1997; Tindall 1997). The case of older persons was discussed in the first chapter and there has been a growth in texts which promote risk taking (Counsel and Care 1993; Lawson 1996; Littlechild and Blakeney 1996; Pritchard 1997; see also the bibliography in Jackson

1992). There is still a tendency to assess for adverse events, such as the risk of falling (see e.g. Hui-Chi *et al.* 2003). Nonetheless, a readier acknowledgement of the need to assess for positive or beneficial outcomes can be found in this literature. Reed (1997) provides a lone voice in questioning both the pro risk and protection schools of thought.

Lay assessments of risk, such as those by service users and family carers, have not been effectively utilised by researchers or, we are entitled to add, by professional assessors themselves. Studies of the differential construction of risks by professionals and service users and their informal carers are, however, now appearing (see e.g. Adams 2001; Clarke 2000). Until more solid research evidence is provided we can only speculate about the contributory factors for positive or negative understandings of risk.

It is worth pointing out that professions such as health promotion specialists are being forced to reconsider their interventions in the light of evidence concerning the very different conceptions of risk that young people, for example, have; for discussions of young people and risk taking, see Aggleton (1996); Cieslik and Pollok (2002) and Moore and Parsons (2000).

All too few research accounts of positive risk assessment, with guidelines to match, may be found in the academic and professional literatures. Alberg *et al.* (1996) do start off with a balanced understanding of risk as quoted above, but the risk assessment guidelines that follow their discussion are based on negative risks, as are the accompanying case studies. Some of the problems evident in the risk assessment literature arise from definitional uncertainty and a failure to clarify with rigour the concept of risk to be deployed. A preoccupation with checklists, often divorced from the values and principles which informed them in the original context, merely adds to the difficulties.

In Chapter 1 we saw that an influential model for risk assessment has been that of Brearley (1982; Pritchard and Brearley 1982). Brearley sought to define risk in terms of 'undesirable' and 'desirable' contingencies, in other words the chance of a loss or a gain, and considered the hazards and strengths involved. A hazard is defined by Brearley as 'any existing factor which introduces or increases the possibility of an undesirable outcome'. A hazard might be the presence of an unscrupulous neighbour who seeks to gain financially from an elderly widower prone to leaving his door open and his wallet on the table. A strength is defined as any factor that reduces the possibility of an undesirable outcome. As Kelly suggests, this 'encouragement to consider and list strengths clearly is of great importance given social workers' natural problem focus' (1996, p.117).

Brearley attempts to improve on his model by differentiating between 'predisposing hazards' and 'situational hazards'. The former (which Kelly prefers to call 'background hazards') are factors of a general nature in a person's background that make an undesirable outcome more likely. It is helpful to pinpoint factors from the background of a person which may increase they stress they are experiencing or which adversely affect their confidence and so have an adverse effect on the outcome. Situational hazards are factors specific to the current circumstances which make an undesirable outcome more likely. This distinction is useful in that it encourages 'decision makers to focus on where the problems are and to focus on those they can alleviate' (Kelly 1996, p.1). However, there is some arbitrariness in allocating which category a particular hazard is assigned to, but the important point is that it is labelled as a hazard.

Brearley suggests that background, situational hazards and strengths can be listed in a grid or columns along with the feared or undesirable outcome, which we can call 'dangers'. This grid can provide a representation of key elements of information needed to make an assessment of risk.

This approach has been taken up by Sheppard (1990) and Prins (1996) for mental health and simplified somewhat by Kelly (1996) for child abuse. The advantage of this approach is that it encourages practitioners to be more analytical in their approach. The problem is that it may lead to 'a simple totting up procedure' where strengths and hazards are totalled and the decision is swayed by the longest list (Kelly 1996, p.118). A disadvantage from the training point of view is that practitioners can get confused by the terms, a finding also noted by Stanley and Manthorpe (1997). A further difficulty identified by Kelly is that it is a static approach and may fail to take into account changes that take place over time. Risk changes over time, place and circumstances, as Grubin (1997) argues.

Finally, background or predisposing factors should not, according to Kelly, be used as the sole determinants in making a decision, but should be used to inform a decision made in relation to current concerns. The importance of dynamic risk assessment has to be emphasised. Brearley's theoretical approach has sterner critics, however, such as Macdonald and Macdonald (1999) who have provided a critique of his treatment of 'probability', 'danger' and 'risk'. They argue that his approach relies on 'slippery concepts' and that a 'definitional haze' obscures the terms he uses (pp.20–21).

One problem is that professionals are presently working with a diversity of guidelines. A reinvention of wheels and a duplication of effort is a notable feature of what does exist. One of the biggest problems is the failure to produce guidance that is linked clearly to a coherent policy framework. Another issue is the growth of assessments involving multi-agency settings and multidisciplinary teams. A major difficulty for such teams is the need for standardised procedures for identification of risk and response among team members; a common checklist approach to iron out inconsistencies in assessment and follow-up has been proposed by Feaviour *et al.* (1995).

The question as to where responsibility lies in multiagency and multidisciplinary settings is increasingly being raised. Kennedy and Gill (1997) posed the question as to whether team members remain equally liable. The writers suggest that while, to take one example, the psychiatrist and social worker are responsible under the mental health legislation, responsibility is less clear in circumstances of voluntary care.

An apparent concentration on risk assessment in the literature is misplaced, according to some authors. This argument takes two main forms in the literature. First, writers such as Carson (1995) argue that the emphasis needs to shift away from an obsession with assessment to the managing of risks. Simply taking as an indicator the size of the literature on the latter, this contention appears to be justified, as will be seen in the next chapter. Second, authors like Wald and Woolverton (1990), writing about the topic of child protection, argue that risk assessment methodologies are deficient and caution against the view that there is a magical solution. Moreover, they criticise the inadequate research basis on which such methodologies rest; as Tomison notes, 'there is currently insufficient information available to determine the efficacy of risk assessment tools for identifying children at risk of serious maltreatment' (1999, p.19). Gambrill and Shlonsky (2000) have also made a similar criticism to that of Wald and Woolverton, arguing that actuarial decision-making in child welfare has been more successful than consensus-based or clinical instrument models. Despite sometimes trenchant criticism (e.g. Saunders and Goddard 1998), many authors in the field of the welfare of children remain, nevertheless, generally supportive of the concept of risk assessment.

'Taking risks', according to Carson, 'involves deciding that the potential benefits of a proposed act outweigh the potential drawbacks' (1988, p.248). The whole process of risk assessment involves this weighing up. Decisions about risks, the Counsel and Care (1993) authors note, are a balance between the right to choice and the competence of the individual. Staff can try to enhance competence, or compensate for it, or offer extra support to allow the individual to do an activity with an acceptable degree of risk.

The central point which should be emphasised is that there should be a clearly understood and shared policy and philosophy to provide a supportive framework for staff and vulnerable individuals alike to make informed decisions about risks, however large or small. Missing from the literatures is a sense that risk taking is a learning experience, involving the sharing of key experiences within and between professions, or between practitioners and service users.

Since the implications for more positive conceptions of risk have rarely been developed, unbalanced assessment frameworks have been produced as a result. A clearer conception of the assessment of risk, in terms of its limits and function, is required. Research accounts have ignored developing risk assessments as a learning experience for practitioners and their clients. Lay assessments of risk have also been neglected, though studies of the construction of risks are appearing (see for example Adams 2001; Clarke 2000).

Risk assessment: contrasting models

Two models of risk assessment, the safety first model and the risk-taking model, can be contrasted. The main characteristics of each are outlined below to illustrate the differences between them. Safety first has traditionally been the dominant model in care for vulnerable people. This approach has been subject to growing criticism (Counsel and Care 1992, 1993; Crosland 1992;). The risk-taking model attempts to build on key principles developed in response to the perceived deficiencies of the first model. The focus of this model is primarily on the *person* and his or her needs. There has to be a balance in looking at what he or she can do, their potential for change and managing their own lives, alongside whatever difficulties he or she might have in day-to-day activities. The risk-taking model allows scope for lay assessment too, and for building on the individual's own understandings and perceptions of risk where this is possible.

Too often professionals work with stereotypes of vulnerable people, such as older people, and what they cannot do. They must look at what the vulnerable person can *achieve* (given the appropriate help) and their potential for change and managing their own lives as far as is practical.

SAFETY-FIRST MODEL

Focus on:

- physical health
- disabilities (what the person *can't* do)
- danger
- control
- what the assessor thinks is right.

RISK-TAKING MODEL

Focus on:

- physical, psychological and emotional well-being
- rights and responsibilities
- abilities and disabilities (what the person *can* achieve)
- choices and opportunities
- involvement of individual and family/carers.

There is a requirement to balance looking at the person's abilities as well as his or her disabilities, what he or she can do alongside whatever difficulties he or she might have. Acceptable risks the vulnerable person can take have to be considered. It is also imperative to think about the person's needs. Stevenson rightly suggests that we need to consider the interaction between need and risk; it is very important that this is 'at the heart of the process' (1999b, p.214). The relationship between need and risk is an intimate one; this is why it is useful to link risk assessments with needs assessments, so that any review of needs takes into account risk taking. This is being done in some fields such as work with juvenile offenders in Canada (Jung and Rawana 1999).

At the heart of good assessment is *communication* – with the person requiring care, with his or her families, friends, neighbours or advocates and with other staff. Learning to talk effectively to people about their needs and wants and the likely consequences of their actions is essential. The secret is to be realistic about what can be achieved: this is all the more important if professionals are working with someone who has had decisions made for them for most of his or her life or who cannot communicate clearly what he or she wants.

The important point is that there should be a clearly understood and shared policy and philosophy to provide a supportive framework for staff and vulnerable individuals alike to make informed decisions about risks, however large or small. Risk assessment can be a valuable learning experience for both practitioners and their clients.

Defining risk assessment

It is important to be clear about what risk assessment is, what it does and what it cannot do. It may be defined, following Brearley (1982) and Alberg *et al.* (1996), as the process of estimating and evaluating risk, understood as the possibility of beneficial and harmful outcomes and the likelihood of their occurrence in a stated timescale. Risk estimation includes: 1. estimating the probability that an outcome will occur and 2. recognising that a number of possible outcomes will occur. Risk evaluation involves attaching a value to each of the identified outcomes and balancing the relative values of each outcome. Risk assessment cannot offer certainty or precision, as emphasised above, but does offer challenges for professional judgement making. Practitioners have to work with the ambiguity which authors like Parton (1998) highlight, but must do so within a systematic and principled approach.

Risk assessment means making judgements about:

- the individual's capabilities and coping resources (social, material and personal)
- the gains for the individual's physical, psychological and emotional well-being

- possible disadvantages and harms
- the values placed on the outcomes
- the consequences for the individual in *not* going ahead with the risk activity.

Parsloe (1999a) helpfully sets out these distinctions in relation to types of risk:

- Risks to service users from other people, usually their own relatives. This is typified by the phrase 'children at risk' but increasingly adults who may be abused are included

- Risks to users themselves from their own behaviour. At its most severe this may mean suicide but it also covers self neglect and perhaps some of the self-endangering behaviour of people with dementia

- Risks to known or unknown others from service users. This category includers 'dangerous parents' but also some offenders and a small number of mentally ill people, especially those who are also substance abusers.

At the outset of this book, it was emphasised that risk considerations pose essential dilemmas for professionals and their colleagues, for people who require care, for their families and kin, as well as for other members of society and their communities. This differentiated nature of risk has implications for its assessment: risks can impact differently at the individual level and at the community level.

With these distinctions and the positive definition from the foregoing discussion in mind, we can consider the main steps involved in assessing risks, identified below. This is broadly based on Carson (n.d.); Counsel and Care (1992, 1993); Lawson (1996) and the discussion contained in Chapters 1 and 2 and the preceding pages.

Key steps in risk assessment
Identify the nature of each risk activity

1. Identify the risk in discussion with all involved.

2. Specify the risk decision to be made (don't be too general or too vague).

Spell out the rationale for each risk activity

Be clear about:

- why the risk activity is proposed
- what will be achieved
- what the justification for the risk is
- what made you stop and think
- what people might say should have been anticipated if things do go wrong
- what exciting things might happen if things go well.

Identify where and when the risk activity will occur

1. Identify the location(s) in which the risks will be incurred (e.g. the street, the home, etc.)
2. Specify the timescale within which the risk activity is to take place.

Identify possible outcomes/benefits and disadvantages

1. List advantages and benefits from taking the risk for:
   - the individual
   - family and friends
   - other people
   - the service.
2. List disadvantages and possible harms which might arise for:
   - the individual
   - family and friends
   - other people
   - the service.
3. Include any opportunities that might be gained or lost.
4. Assign values placed on each of the benefits and harms by:
   - the individual
   - the assessor

   i.e. what importance is attached to each of the identified benefits and harms according to the main parties to the risk decision?

Estimate likelihood of risk

1. Estimate the likelihood of each type of harm within the specified time frame to:

    • the individual

    • family and friends

    • other people

    • the service.

2. Decide on the likelihood of each harm within the specified time frame to see if it is:

    (a) unlikely to happen

    (b) may happen or

    (c) very likely to happen.

Compile risk / individual profile

For more complex cases and/or where there is a desire or potential to undertake a range of risk activities. These risk activities and risk situations should be matched against a profile of the capabilities and coping resources of the individual. The coping resources which should be considered include:

    • personal resources

    • social resources

    • material resources.

This analysis can also be combined with risk factors at different levels, for example profiles of communities at risk (such as an area of social stress or multiple deprivation or with significant health inequalities).

Following the first five steps outlined above should allow welfare workers and others systematically to examine and review the key factors relevant for many of their risk decisions. The sixth step is intended for instances of a more complicated nature, for example where there is much uncertainty about an individual's ability to cope in a time of major transition, e.g. when moving from a hostel to an independent flat, and where there is a range of risk situations to consider.

Risk plans

Some agencies have been developing risk analysis sheets or assessment forms which can act as valuable aids to risk decision making. They provide a record of the steps followed, decisions reached and dates for review. More than that however, they can provide a basis for a written statement on risk taking which the individual, his or her informal carers, assessor(s) and care staff can sign up to. This in effect provides a risk plan for the individual: an example which combines key steps for assessment and management is provided in Appendix 2.

Conclusion

In this chapter we reviewed the literature on risk assessment, which was found wanting in a number of respects. In particular, it is fair to conclude that there is a preoccupation with negative risks and adverse outcomes, with a corresponding lack of emphasis on assessment for positive risks and beneficial outcomes. Two contrasting models for assessment were compared, the risk-taking and the safety-first models, with the latter being criticised for its limited focus on danger and control. A definition of risk assessment was unpacked into its elements of estimation and evaluation, and guidance for welfare professionals undertaking risk assessment was provided in the form of key steps. In Chapter 6, the discussion moves on to consider the next stage, risk management.

Risk Management

Introduction

Risk management constitutes an important activity for welfare professionals and their managers but it is all too often overshadowed by the attention
given to risk assessment. The aim of this chapter is to redress the balance
and set out some guidance for professionals, other carers and users
involved in the risk-taking process. Having reviewed the literature and set
out the key steps for risk assessment in the previous chapter, we shall do
the same for risk management in this chapter. Once again the discussion
begins with a review of some of the existing literature on the topic;
however, the body of relevant work is not a large one. We shall then set out
key steps for managing risks, a main stage in the PRAMS approach
described in Chapter 4.

The literature on risk management

Compared with risk assessment, risk management in health and social care
has received much less attention in the literature. In part this is a reflection
of the priority given to risk assessment in professional work; this has led to
an unbalanced approach where insufficient attention is paid to the management of risk. Writing about the lessons from recent inquiries into homicides involving people with serious mental illness, Reed writes that 'risk
assessment alone is not enough; it must be accompanied by a risk management plan which includes review procedures' (1997, p.5). He also highlights issues for interagency working and information sharing.

A key difficulty with the existing literature is that identified by authors such as Ryan (1996) who argue that risk management is often seen as minimising risk. Ryan then explicitly proceeds to deal with risk minimisation as synonymous with management of danger to the public. However, in his more recent writing exploring the risk management strategies of mental health service users, he uses users' own views about managing their illness in proactive ways (Ryan 2000). The problem of limited definition is particularly pronounced in the field of mental health (see e.g. Mental Health Reference Group 2000; Morgan 2000; Munson 1996; O'Rourke and Bird 2001), where models such as the Care Programme Approach have been based on a restrictive view of risk (Harrison 1997).

A different, and potentially more radical, view has been emerging, according to Davis (1996), and this is the risk-taking approach; this has been developed by practitioners with an explicit agenda to involve and empower mental health service users with a more positive perception of risk. For Davis, these two approaches provide 'contrasting orientations to risk' for social workers (1996, p.116). Risk minimisation, in Davis's eyes, is about the surveillance and control of a small number of dangerous people. In contrast, the approach which emphasises risk taking involves encouraging participation in society and promoting values such as choice and autonomy.

Clarke and Heyman, looking at risk management for people with dementia, argue that 'minimising one risk frequently exacerbates another' (1998, p.239). They contend that more effective strategies can be developed where there is an acknowledgement that professionals and family carers approach risk from different perspectives. Dementia looks quite different from the viewpoint of family carers compared to professional views. By emphasising the physical and psychological risks faced by the family carers, the professionals are 'implicitly writing off the humanity of the person with dementia' (1998, p.238). The keys to more effective managment are a shared understanding of the differences on views of risk, partnership and a willingness to accommodate. More recently, Clarke (2000) has explored different constructions of risk and dementia among practitioners, carers and those with dementia.

Negative and limited understandings of the management of risk dominate the literature. This can be most readily seen in the mental health field, which Soltys argues has 'unique risk management challenges' (1995, p.473; see also Kaliski 1997). Soltys cites and makes use of Reed and Swain's definition of risk management as the 'systematic...effort to eliminate or reduce harm to persons and the threat of financial losses' (p.473). Secker-Walker (1997, p.367), writing in a similar vein about health care, focuses on the need for a framework which addresses the 'varied causes of latent and active human failure'. The Royal Society (1992) has also produced a rather limited concept of the potential of risk management. The Health and Safety Executive (HSE), and the health and safety literature in general, also tend to operate with a negative and restricted understanding of risk management, defined largely in terms of hazard or harm minimisation (for example Health and Safety Executive 1997, 1998).

Issue has already been taken with the definition by Alaszewski *et al.* (1998) of risk management as collective or group responses to risk; these authors neglect the opportunity to explore in greater depth conceptions of risk management and what is entailed in the process. The need to connect risk assessment and management has been recognised by Smith (1997) for the probation service, for the mental health field by Davison (1997) and by Halstead (1997) for learning disability.

Holloway (1997) made a request for the development of management strategies in psychiatry, but particularly with a view to discourage inadequate staffing in inpatient units and devolution of responsibility to staff who are not adequately trained or properly supported. Darr (1999) argued that links must be made to the improvement of quality. In the field of probation, similar arguments have been made for the importance of risk management (Nash 1998); see also Scheflin (1998) on treating child sexual abuse; McLennan *et al.* (1998) for illegal drug users; Strand *et al.* (1999) for mentally disordered offenders; and Gambrill and Shlonsky (2001) on risk management systems in the area of child welfare.

Tanner criticises the concept of risk management as 'concerned with identification and management of social problems rather than their treatment' (1998, p.16). This criticism has some validity when the debate of managing people in the mental health field is examined. It should remind professionals not to lose sight of individuals and their needs and not subsume them under the guise of identifying and managing social problems. This is part of the problem with the language of 'risk management', which in the literature tends to lend itself to the defining and labelling of socially constructed problems (Manning 1987). The tension between risk management in its restrictive sense and potentially empowering approaches (see e.g. Kemshall 2002b; Stalker 2003) was mentioned in the first chapter. How risk can be used to empower vulnerable individuals has, unfortunately, received insufficient attention in the literature.

The emergence of the clinical governance agenda has meant a growing concern with the management of risk among managers and professionals in the health field (Cowan 2003; Harris 2000). Clinical governance was introduced into the NHS in 1998 in an attempt to improve the Government's strategy on clinical effectiveness. Studies of attitudes towards risk management found that front-line professionals are often not keen to report adverse events, especially where no harm has occured to the patient (Wallace, Boxall and Spurgeon 2004). The development of clinical governance is intended to develop corporate responsibility and use support and training to improve learning from incidents and from best practice. However, the management of risk is often simply conceived in terms of the reduction of errors.

It is hard to find a view of risk management which encompasses achievement as well as failure. The research literature has little to say about the limits of risk management; its stages, including where assessment stops and management starts; practical guidance about intervention and, importantly, when not to intervene. Lawson (1996) rightly notes that risk management is not equivalent to getting rid of risk: risk will always continue and a process has to be developed for its management. Using the example of older people, she suggests that risk management issues should be included in care plans and care programmes.

As Tindall (1997) points out, it can also provide a more systematic way for helping people with learning difficulties take more control over their lives. Risk management is particularly important in breaking consistently reinforced low expectations and assisting personal development; it ensures advance planning. It offers the opportunity for staff to protect themselves but it also provides opportunities for the empowerment of people with learning disabilities. Therefore all efforts to manage risk should have the wishes and needs of the individual person with learning disabilities as the main consideration. The aim of a successful management process, Tindall argues, should be to 'maximise opportunities for people with learning disabilities to take risks which are carefully assessed and planned in order that they can maintain a good quality of life, develop new skills or try previously untried experiences' (1997, p.107). High quality risk management is marked out by the attention given to the needs and wishes of the individual, and the agreed plan of action for reducing harm should respect the rights of the individual as a citizen.

The management of risk

The aim should be to increase benefits, as well as minimising harms, and this needs to be emphasised in training for managers and practitioners. Managing risk in the lives of vulnerable people, then, should not mean eliminating risk. This would run counter to the whole philosophy which is being advocated in the risk-taking model. Instead it means providing a *process* for ensuring that potential benefits identified by the risk assessment are increased and that the likelihood of harms occurring as a result of taking a risk are reduced.

Risk management, moreover, does not mean anticipating every single potential risk and responding accordingly. This would be impossible and again would run counter to the risk-taking approach. Instead it entails developing a systematic approach which allows for the planning of risk-taking strategies and for monitoring and reviewing. A sound risk management process will help to ensure accountability, clarity and support for staff involved in decisions concerning risk. The process of managing risks must both facilitate risk taking and empower care professionals to make important decisions. What it should do is place risk management issues at the heart of considerations in the assessment of health and social care needs, care plans and care programmes.

The management of risk, as Littlechild and Blakeney (1996) state, must be adaptable. People do not stay constant; changes can take place in the ability to cope. The risks can change too. Monitoring is important to keep abreast of any such changes. This involves working closely with the individual, with their family and carers and with other care staff. Everyone should have a clear idea of what the main risks are and what can be done about them. This is about clarifying expectations and arriving at a realistic, negotiated understanding of risks and how they can be managed. This is where the professional expertise of the welfare worker needs to be focused: *not* on a futile attempt to identify every single potential problem and to control the situation to reduce every single danger.

In summary, the key points emerging from this discussion are these. Risk management is more than simply risk minimisation. It entails efforts to increase potential benefits and to provide a process for planning risk-taking strategies and for monitoring and reviewing the results. Any risk management process must be both flexible and adaptable. A major challenge will be in promoting achievement-oriented visions of risk management.

The secret of a good risk management process is this:

Risk management = Process of compromise and negotiation.

Key steps for risk management

To develop a systematic process for the management of risks, we should be prepared to go through the key steps which are identified below.

Consult and communicate

There needs to be a process of communication with everyone involved: be prepared for negotiation and compromise on all sides. Consultation with all involved is essential in order to reach clear and shared understandings. As Ryan (1997) notes, communication between professionals is the main factor in many of the recent inquiries about people with serious mental health needs.

Prepare risk plan

Plans are not essential for everyone but for many vulnerable people they can be helpful and can provide a framework for professionals and the individual to work within. There should be an individual risk plan (linked to the care plan) which is clear and agreed and where the main risks are spelled out as far as is practical and written down. The plan should include clear statements on:

- who has been consulted
- who is responsible for planning and implementation
- the steps that will be taken to minimise possible harms

- the steps to be taken to enhance possible benefits
- agreed timescales
- the points at which intervention would occur and how this will happen
- the milestones for measuring success or failure
- arrangements for record keeping.

Sign up

This should be a 'signing up' process where the individual, his or her family and formal and informal carers are fully aware of the risk assessment and risk decisions. All parties to the risk decision should provide their signatures with dates attached. This is an important step since it is about sharing the ownership of the risk decision. Lawson (1996) suggests that this can readily be done in care plans and care programmes. 'In this way', she writes, 'users and carers (both formal and informal) will wherever possible have signed up to and be fully aware of the risk assessment and decisions' (p.65). They will therefore have more realistic expectations of each other.

Share information

An information strategy for managing the risks is essential: everyone involved must be prepared to share information and maintain awareness. Tindall (1997) suggests that agencies should build into their risk management process the capacity to gather information in the light of the risk assessment and to disseminate examples of good practice across staff teams as part of a wider quality assurance process. The Department of Health (1996) and Ryan (1997) advocate that networks of relationships needs to be developed between professionals to help in the exchange of information. A common complaint which arises in training sessions concerns the lack of passing on of information, with statutory authorities not keeping voluntary authorities informed and vice versa.

Monitor and review

Provision must be made for regular monitoring and reviewing: the frequency of reviews, intensity of monitoring and extent to which other staff and agencies are involved should be made clear and written down. Authors such as Lawson (1996) emphasise the importance of reviewing, particularly in defining time limits for the reviews.

Support staff

Support and supervisory arrangements for staff involved in making difficult risk decisions should be clearly spelled out. It is vital that staff are given support when there is an adverse outcome to the risk decision.

As Lawson (1996) notes, it is important for the worker to have an opportunity to share thoughts with a senior member of staff in supervision. Risk assessment and management is an area where workers feel stressed and under pressure to make decisions. The supervisory process can help to alleviate this pressure and provide feedback and guidance for staff. Tindall (1997, p.104) argues that 'adequate debriefing and reparation should follow any risk which had a negative outcome'.

Conclusion

In this chapter the relevant literature has been criticised for its obsession with risk management simply as harm minimisation and for the lack of a positive vision of risk management. Risk management strategies have to be broadened to take account of the developing and boosting of the positive features of the risk situation and to build on the vulnerable person's coping skills. Steps to guide the risk management process were presented. The issue of how risk assessment and management can be linked together now needs to be considered, and forms the subject of the next chapter, where we try to fit the different pieces into a single framework.

Chapter 7

Linking Risk Assessment and Management

Introduction

In this chapter we shall attempt to bring together all the elements outlined in the preceding chapters to form a framework for risk taking, and to take an overview of the PRAMS system and look at some of the issues involved. In particular, there is a focus on linking risk assessment and risk management together within a coherent framework. There is also a consideration of the issue of support for professionals involved in risk decisions. We noted earlier that a number of writers have called for more explicit links between assessment and management (for example Davison 1997; Smith 1997). It was argued particularly that these links need to be considerably strengthened if a joined-up approach to risk taking is to take place.

Linking risk assessment and risk management

Figure 7.1 is an attempt to provide a flowchart of the main stages in risk assessment and risk management. It is strongly recommended that assessment and management be considered as discrete but interrelated activities. The flowchart is based on the discussion in Chapters 5 and 6 and on Counsel and Care (1992, 1993) and Lawson (1996). The flowchart provides a summary of the main stages which should be followed in making a risk decision. Counsel and Care (1992) usefully raised the idea that principles are needed, along with a 'framework within which staff have some safety to take risks and allow risks in their clients'.

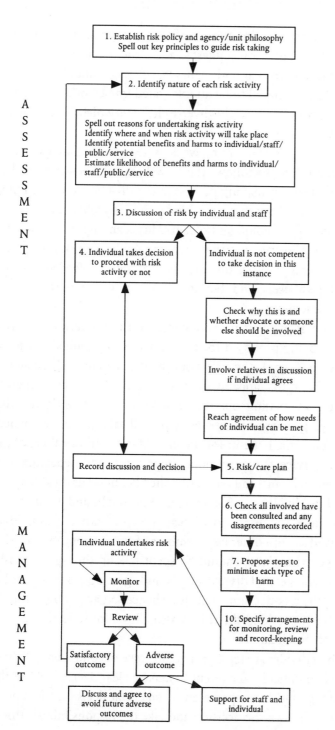

A
S
S
E
S
S
M
E
N
T

M
A
N
A
G
E
M
E
N
T

1. Establish risk policy and agency/unit philosophy
Spell out key principles to guide risk taking

2. Identify nature of each risk activity

Spell out reasons for undertaking risk activity
Identify where and when risk activity will take place
Identify potential benefits and harms to individual/staff/
public/service
Estimate likelihood of benefits and harms to individual/
staff/public/service

3. Discussion of risk by individual and staff

4. Individual takes decision to proceed with risk activity or not

Individual is not competent to take decision in this instance

Check why this is and whether advocate or someone else should be involved

Involve relatives in discussion if individual agrees

Reach agreement of how needs of individual can be met

Record discussion and decision

5. Risk/care plan

6. Check all involved have been consulted and any disagreements recorded

Individual undertakes risk activity

Monitor

Review

7. Propose steps to minimise each type of harm

10. Specify arrangements for monitoring, review and record-keeping

Satisfactory outcome

Adverse outcome

Discuss and agree to avoid future adverse outcomes

Support for staff and individual

Figure 7.1: Person-centred risk assessment and management system

In the previous chapter the importance of risk management as a separate stage was considered, but it was suggested at the end that there is a need to consider how the asssessment and management stages should be linked together. PRAMS is intended to be an integrated framework, so a central element now is to consider how the diverse elements which have been discussed can best fit together.

The first task is to set out a framework as a series of related steps for professionals and others to follow; the flowchart has been provided to illustrate the risk decision-making process in the PRAMS system. At Step 1, it is necessary to spell out the risk-taking policy at agency level and/or at the level of the unit or community team. This is an important stage for setting out the key principles which we want to guide our risk taking. It is worth investing at this point: getting members of staff involved along with managers, and also users and family carers, in broadening out the ownership of risk issues.

At Step 2 the assessment phase commences; the nature of the risk activity which is being proposed for the vulnerable individual has to be identified. Next, in Step 3, the risk assessment schedule as discussed in Chapter 5 can be systematically gone through. This is conveniently summarised here as spelling out the reasons for undertaking the risk activity; identifying where the risk activity will take place, and when; identifying the potential benefits for the individual, staff, members of the public and the service the practitioner represents, and repeating this process for potential harms; and estimating the likelihood of these benefits and harms for the individual, staff, members of the public and the service.

For Step 4, it is important to discuss the risk with the individual concerned, as well as with other key members of staff as appropriate. This is a crucial stage, where time should be spent talking through the risks involved, the advantages and disadvantages, and agreeing as far as possible broad limits for the risk decision. This is a chance to gauge how strongly the person feels about taking the risk; it also allows for reflection on the pros and cons of the situation.

The flowchart divides at Step 4 around the issue of competency. Where the vulnerable individual is competent to make a clear decision about the risk, the person should be empowered to take that decision for him or herself. They should own the decision and take the responsibility – this is what ownership means. If all goes well the discussion and the risk decision is recorded.

If the individual is judged not to be competent to take a decision in this particular instance, steps should be taken to check why this is the case. A decision has to be made about whether an advocate or someone else should be involved in the risk decision. It may be appropriate to involve relatives in the discussion if the individual agrees. At this stage agreement on how the needs of the person can best be met has to be thrashed out.

Step 5 involves setting up a risk plan or coordinating risks of the plan which has been arranged or which is being discussed. Hence the key elements for the plan as outlined in Chapter 6 need to be considered. The elements should be familiar to most workers who have to work with care plans and the CPA type approach. However, it is not necessary to have a plan; as indicated in the previous chapter not everyone needs a formal plan.

Step 6 entails that all parties to the risk decision have been consulted. This will include final discussions of the decision and trying, as far as is possible, to reach a consensus on an agreement of the risk decision. Where it proves impossible to secure everyone's agreement, these disagreements can be recorded.

Thereafter it is essential at Step 7 to set out the key actions designed to minimise each type of harm identified by the risk assessment. It is also important not to neglect the benefits which the assessment will have identified above; steps which will increase the likelihood of positive outcomes happening should now be proposed.

At Step 8 arrangements for monitoring, reviewing and the keeping of records have to be specified. It should be a requirement to ensure that these are in place first before risk taking occurs.

At the next step of the flowchart, Step 9, the individual begins the process of undertaking the risk activity identified in Steps 2 to 4 in the assessment. It is now important to monitor how the individual is doing and how he or she is coping. A review is essential and an agreed date should be set. This forms Step 10.

If there is a satisfactory outcome, practitioners should reflect and learn from this success, along with the person concerned. The questions they need to ask are: what went well and why?

If there is an adverse outcome, if harm results or something goes wrong, again it is essential to stop and learn from the mistakes. This is an important part of the learning process. The need for discussion and agreement on how to avoid future adverse outcomes is paramount. Crucially, support needs to be provided both for the staff involved and for the individual. Equally important however, the next step involves being prepared to return to the top of the flowchart again, to learn from the past and move on to take more risks. Slow steps can be taken to build up the confidence of the vulnerable individual.

Risk taking and support for professionals and vulnerable people

People in caring services need support in the process of taking risks, otherwise their capacity to take risks will be diminished and they will lose the creativity they bring to the task. As Norman (1987) notes, a more relaxed regime puts maximum reliance on individual staff judgements and capacity for accepting responsibility for use of time and mode of delivering care. The authors of *What If They Hurt Themselves?* make an important point about the relationship between risk taking and support for staff:

> Those operating in caring services are often placed in situations in which the risks they take can jeopardise the people for whom they have responsibility. They need support in this process of taking risks, and even more when the risks they have taken lead to unpredicted results. *Without such backing*, their capacity to take risks will be diminished and with that will be lost the creativity they bring to the task. (Counsel and Care 1992, p.12, emphasis added)

However, it is not just professional workers who require support but also the vulnerable persons taking the risk, as well as their family carers, a point which has been emphasised throughout this book. Davis (1996) states that organisational support is essential if risk work is to be balanced and effective. Organisations provide the mandate for the work undertaken by, for example, mental health social work practitioners, and they also have responsibilities in relation to the fulfilment of that mandate. As Davis perceptively notes, 'practitioners who are anxious and defensive because of their perceptions that they need to act in ways which protect them from organisational blame are unlikely to meet the requirements of good practice in this area' (1996, p.118). Regular supervision is essential, a point also stressed by Lawson (1996).

Conclusion

Building the links between assessment and management is essential, as is designing in all the essential stages of a system which purports to promote risk taking. In this chapter a framework for risk taking was set out, consisting of the PRAMS system, which links together risk assessment and risk management and which provides the necessary stages. A flowchart, Figure 7.1, outlined the main steps for managers, professionals and vulnerable individuals to follow. Finally, the importance of support and a supportive environment for practitioners and for vulnerable people was emphasised. The presence of both a coherent framework and a supportive environment will considerably enhance the prospects of success in promoting creative approaches to risk in welfare settings.

Chapter 8

Training Professionals and Laypersons in Risk Taking

Introduction

A major challenge in the promotion of risk-taking approaches is the development of training for welfare professionals, as well as for communities, including vulnerable individuals, their families and relatives and other carers. In this chapter we examine issues for the training of these professionals and laypersons such as services users and informal carers in risk taking. The role of research, particularly in relation to the impact and effectiveness of training, is also considered. The results of various evaluations and studies carried out by the author are presented for discussion, and finally, some suggestions for training professionals and vulnerable people in the area of risk decision making are put forward.

Training professionals in risk work

The literature has little to say about the effectiveness of training professionals in risk work with vulnerable people (Titterton 1999); as Parsloe argues, 'there is virtually no research' on the effect of staff training on assessment and management (1999a, p.7). There are some general writings on health and safety issues (Corfield 1994; Murphy 1996; Oakley and Taylor 1994; Toye 1992). A steadily growing body of work on training effectiveness and evaluation also exists (Fowler 1993; Oliver and Scott 1996; Pearce 1995, 1997; Rae 1986, 1995; Talbot 1992). Walton (1978) explores some of the issues of training staff in residential care in taking risks. Stanley and Manthorpe (1997) also present an account of a short training course in risk assessment in mental health work. They contend that risk assessment can strengthen communication between professionals and others. However the impacts of the training were not explored by the writers. More recently, Wall, Eynon and Bullock (2000) have evaluated a series of modules for clinical risk management training in the West Midlands and Lefevre, Waters and Budetti (2000) have surveyed training programmes in risk management in terms of communication skills.

Many calls for training have emerged from inquiries (e.g. North West London Mental Health NHS Trust 1994; Ritchie, Dick and Lingham 1994) as Stanley and Manthorpe (1997) note, and from other literature (Harrison 1997). Reed claims, in his review of the lessons from recent inquiries, that '(a)ll these reasons for failure are, essentially, amenable to better training – and particularly training in a multidisciplinary, multiagency setting' (1997, p.6). He pinpoints the areas of risk assessment, the use of the Mental Health Acts and the use of security. This is sometimes targeted towards particular groups such as key workers. Harrison advocates a modularised curriculum which is 'applicable to all professional groups' (1997, p.39).

There is little of substance in the literature concerning the kinds of training, including methods and formats, which work most effectively with different kinds of professionals, though Wall *et al.* (2000) have some suggestions to make about the organisation of training in relation to clinical risk management. The issue of the training of trainers is clearly an important one but there is also a pronounced lacuna. Harris (1997) looks at this problem in relation to psychiatrists. He raises a concern about the wide variation in the ability of trainers to do formal teaching and a lack of training in the methods of teaching; he also claims there is a lack of audit of the effectiveness of the training. Harris points to the value of including other professionals in this training, such as community psychiatric nurses. He limits himself to three methods, lectures, seminars and national conferences, which represent a limited view of training methods.

Translating research findings in the area of risk assessment into the daily practice of professionals can pose problems, as Taylor and Meux (1997) have noted. These authors point out, for example, that different clinicians will interpret research findings differently and act differently in risk assessment and management, since they are individuals whose judgements are shaped by temperament, experiences and professional backgrounds. This argument can be extended to other professionals such as social workers, who rely on similarly fine judgements. The authors also argue that decisions will also be affected by factors such as culture, health care and legal systems and the availability of resources. Taylor and Meux deploy a case vignette method to compare and contrast approaches to risk assessment in psychiatry by three different professionals from different countries for each of three case studies. Their findings indicated that despite the variety of professional and national backgrounds all recognised some degree of risk, but there were differences of emphasis which 'illustrate again that aspect of risk management which can never be under-emphasised: the importance of a multidisciplinary input' (1997, p.301). The importance of multidisciplinary and multiagency training for practitioners and managers across a range of settings using imaginative formats, as emphasised by Titterton (1994), is underlined by their research.

Social work competences in relation to risk work have yet to be properly researched and discussed within the literature: a collection on the topic of competences by Vass (1996) contained no references to risk work in its index. Some of the core competences for social workers were pinpointed by Kelly (1996), for example those advocated by the Central Council for Education and Training in Social Work (CCETSW) Revised Paper 30; these include assessing and planning, communicating and engaging and so on (CCETSW 1996). A more explicit acknowledgement of the specific kinds of competences required for risk work (reflected in the sort of skills which are discussed in the second part of this chapter) was called for. As Alaszewksi and Manthorpe (1991) noted, the lack of clear recognition by CCETSW was reflected in the absence of discussion in general social work texts.

The growing emphasis by bodies such as the Scottish Social Services Council on risk assessment and management as part of social services workers' practice (Scottish Social Services Council 2003) and by the Scottish Executive (2003) as part of the Scottish Requirements for Social Work Training, is set out in *The Framework for Social Work Education in Scotland*. Though more detail is provided, this is equivalent to the Department of Health's *Requirements for Social Work Training*, set in train by the Care Standards Act 2000 (Department of Health 2002). The

Standards in Social Work Education set out what student social workers will need to achieve to gain the honours degree and to become professionally qualified (Scottish Executive 2003); Northern Ireland has also outlined a specification for its degree and is reviewing the post-qualifying framework (Department of Health, Social Services and Public Safety 2003). The standards combine the principal elements of two previous standards documents for social work: the Quality Assurance Agency for Higher Education's Benchmark Statement and the National Occupational Standards for Social Work. One standard is identified as 'assess and manage risk to individuals, families, carers, groups, communities, self and colleagues', similar to Key Role 4 in the English document (Department of Health 2002). A useful start on explicitly recognising some of the main competences has been made for social work education as a whole. These include statements such as 'identify, understand and critically evaluate ethical issues, dilemmas and conflicts affecting practice'. This setting out of the main standards and competences chimes closely with the PRAMS approach described in earlier chapters. However, the specific types of competences needed for high quality risk work remain to be more clearly spelled out, along with the implications for appropriate learning structures and opportunities.

The front-line worker, Burke (1999) notes, is responsible for assessing clients and offering an appropriate and skilled service to those in need. Some workers find this difficult and some may not be able to distinguish between the different needs of users. The skills of the worker need to be linked to the needs of the client. Supervision of a skilled nature is required here. Social workers need to develop their 'practice wisdom' and supervision can help in this respect; the role supervision can play in assisting workers in risk management was noted in Chapter 6.

Training of professionals is often advocated as the answer to problems associated with risk situations with potentially adverse outcomes (Titterton 1999). Big expectations are increasingly being placed on training, at a time when training budgets have not been well protected in the health and social services. Training has to be seen as part of a process of learning over time. The trainer will often provide the trainee with helpful reference points for the start of this process. But, as argued elsewhere (Titterton 1999), training must be recognised as only one piece of the bigger picture that constitutes good practice in risk work. Other pieces include: the development of risk policies; the involvement of informal carers and users; the influencing of professional standards and expectations and the changing of public and media perceptions of risks. In addition, a range of organisational issues (Alaszewski and Manthorpe 1998; Kemshall *et al.* 1997), and a wider set of cultural and political factors (Franklin 1998) must be taken into consideration.

Description of the training

From the preceding discussion it is clear that there is an urgent need to find out more about appropriate training methodologies in risk work and their effectiveness. We go on to consider the effectiveness of one approach to training and developmental work with social work and other staff. The PRAMS model has already been outlined; this forms the basis of a training course devised by the author. It has been developed on the basis of research and consultation, and over a thousand professionals have participated in Scotland and outside Scotland, including both carers and users in workshop sessions. The learning objectives of the course are:

- to examine issues of risk-taking
- to explore ways of assessing and managing risks
- to develop a multiagency awareness
- to provide guidance for managers, workers, users and their carers
- to help increase choice in the daily lives of service users.

Evaluation of the training

The great majority of participants who completed an evaluation form after the course outlined above felt it met the aims and objectives stipulated and found it enjoyable and challenging. However, some did not feel it was long enough, particularly the short (one-day) version of the course, since the difficult dilemmas which were emerging needed longer time for discussion. They enjoyed coming together and learning together; it is evidently important that the training format encourages this. Participants benefited not only from working in small groups with colleagues but also working with those from different settings and dealing with different care groups.

What participants found most helpful were a logical and systematic approach to risk assessment and management; a clear focus on practical understanding; exchanging ideas and well structured and well presented information. They also enjoyed listening to different views of risk and the involvement of different professions. Participants also reported that they enjoyed risk planning; learning how to develop an effective policy; defining boundaries between risk assessment and risk management; considering the right to take risks and treating people as individuals; not being afraid to take risks and thinking through the issues. Case studies, group work and the training manual for further reference were also identified as helpful.

The aspects which some training participants found least helpful were the negativity of some people who were not prepared to take risks; people raising issues specific to their workplace; grey areas and boundaries and a mix of backgrounds making it hard to discuss specific issues. However, there were other respondents who evidently found the latter two situations useful.

Other points raised by participants were that senior managers also needed training; training needs to be on a continuing basis; managers need to discuss policy expectations with workers; agreements on confidentiality were needed. There was also a demand for involving the different sectors in training: social work, health, housing and voluntary. Participants also wanted feedback on cases where something 'goes wrong', as well as support of workers by managers on these occasions.

The follow-up evaluation

Research was carried out to examine the longer-term impact of the training on professionals and the individuals they look after. The following analysis is based on 40 completed returns from a self-completion questionnaire distributed to social work, health and housing professionals who had attended the course in the preceding nine months. Respondents were asked about the effects of the training in a number of areas. The first of these concerned the impact on practice. How far was the training incorporated and what examples could they provide? Next, what effects did the training have on their clients? Again, could any examples be provided? They were then asked about obstacles to taking risks. A question was also posed about other training or support which might be useful. Finally, they were asked to comment on the difficulties in involving users in risk decisions.

The impact on practice

The respondents for the most part suggested that the training had made a 'substantial impact' on practice. This can be divided into effects on individual practice and on agency practice. Comments on individual practice included: 'forces you to work through things in a logical order'; it 'made me more confident in dealing with other professions, made me feel more secure'; it 'allowed me to view risk in a new light' and encouraged the assessing of positive benefits as well as dangers.

Comments on agency practice included: 'found the key steps a very useful tool in carrying out assessments'. Some informants noted that the benefits of training were being passed on to others in the agency and in some, follow-up training was being planned; others reported the production of informal guidelines; others stated that there was a search for consensus on risk taking in multidisciplinary settings, as well as for ways of dealing with conflicting views. Consideration of risk was reported by at least one informant as being a regular part of discussions about and with service users. Some others stated that their agency's definition of risk was being broadened to include more positive risk taking.

The effect on clients

A small number reported that it was still 'early days' for risk taking; others were prepared to comment about the effect on clients. One of the social workers noted that a risk-taking approach, developed following the training, 'has helped build self-esteem and confidence' and another that her 'client is more relaxed, with a more positive attitude and awareness'. One of the most notable findings was that some social workers and care staff claimed to be involving clients more and consciously making efforts to allow them to take decisions, pointing out the consequences of actions but encouraging them to feel in control. Another worker stated that he was 'now more likely to ask service users to identify risks for themselves' and to work with users' perceptions of risks.

Some respondents said their clients were making more choices for themselves. One support worker pointed to an example of a young female tenant having more control over budgeting and shopping; the tenant was occasionally overspending and getting into debt which may lead to the decision being reviewed in the future, but the worker still felt it was right to allow the young person to try to manage by herself.

One respondent gave the example of a client assuming a role supporting others in a project and becoming more confident, which was seen as important for the individual's self-development; another used the example of a young man with learning disabilities and severe epilepsy being encouraged to do more with less supervision, while yet another pointed to the example of an older client taking risks with cooking. More than one informant pointed out that calculated risk taking was boosting the self-esteem and confidence of their client. A few respondents emphasised that this approach was no easy option and, in the words of one, that it is 'difficult to move with some clients and carers'.

Obstacles to risk taking

A small number of informants stressed that there were no obstacles to risk taking in their work settings, and noted that they had good management support. However, this appeared to be a minority view, with most replies detailing a number of barriers. These can be grouped into four main categories.

First, respondents pointed to general fears about letting people make choices, and here cultural and professional factors were implicated. One social worker complained about 'the tendency to wrap people in cotton wool', while a housing support worker wrote about 'our own fears of letting tenants take risks'. Second, the lack of support from management was identified as a major stumbling block. Third, differences between professionals and the lack of a shared enterprise between disciplines were highlighted. More than one person asked for more joint training, for example involving home care and health care professionals such as GPs, consultants, and hospital staff, as well as more training 'at different levels'. Fourth, organisational factors were cited: one informant noted that the 'culture of the organisation' can militate against a risk-taking approach, with another arguing that the 'whole organisation needs to take on risk taking' before it can succeed.

In addition, a range of miscellaneous factors was identified. Difficulties in devising standardised policies due to the diversity of clients and their needs and abilities were mentioned. Some pointed to problems with registration and inspection staff who were reluctant to countenance risk taking, as well as 'difficult parents'. One person wrote that a key barrier was the attitude that 'staff were there just to "look after" and not to let people face risks'. Others stated that senior management tend to have a more reactive approach to risk and one respondent complained of the 'feeling of being out on a limb' when taking a risk decision. The influence of the media was commonly cited as an obstacle.

Key skills for risk assessment and risk management

Many of the skills required for risk assessment and risk management will be familiar from other areas where good practice is required, e.g. effective communication. Kelly (1996) highlighted some of the core competences for social workers, those required by CCETSW's Revised Paper 30; these included assessing and planning, communicating and engaging and so on. Some mentioned 'risk' directly, such as 'work in partnership to assess and review people's circumstances and plan response to need and risk'. In *The Framework for Social Work Education in Scotland*, the Standards in Social Work Education include a wide range of 'transferable skills', from active listening through to research skills (Scottish Executive 2003; see also the Department of Health 2002). Again, those skills relevant for high quality risk work require to be more explicitly addressed by researchers and educators.

In the research described above on the PRAMS training model, respondents were asked about the kinds of skills which they felt were important for developing risk-taking approaches. The first group of skills involved communication skills, such as the 'ability to communicate risk calculation effectively to others, and provide support for risk taking partnerships'. One informant noted that 'the word "risk" is alarming for staff and clients', while another identified the need to put over issues in a way which clients can understand as essential, and yet another emphasised the importance of getting family and friends to see the benefits of risk decisions.

A second set of skills involved 'identifying what risks are and what has made them risks'; judging risks and weighing up benefits; analysing risky situations; cultivating new ways of thinking for risk taking; 'thinking things through in greater depth' and developing the ability to look at the consequences of decisions in a long-term perspective.

Another group of skills consisted of interprofessional and interagency skills, including working with other professionals on risk decisions and, in the words of one informant, 'how to convey our perception of risk to other agencies'. A fourth set concerned planning skills such as forward planning and developing suitable risk plans, as well as the writing of and documentation of plans. The final cluster can be termed negotiation skills, such as balancing the various, and sometimes conflicting, rights of clients and their carers and reaching agreements over decisions about risks.

Other training and support required

Respondents made a variety of comments under this heading. Some made clear a desire to expand the basis of the training, with comments such as the 'whole organisation needs to get involved'. Joint training was commonly cited as a potentially valuable exercise, for practitioners and managers alike. There was a demand to know more about 'what works and what does not work'. One informant advocated workshops to allow people working in similar situations and with similar clients to discuss issues. Some requested updates on the risk-taking practices of other staff: what they have found and what the clients' views have been afterwards.

Further training was identified as desirable in specific areas: individual support and risk plans; overcoming difficulties in securing risk decisions and agreements; recording; group leadership skills; and helping clients develop risk-taking skills.

Finally, continuing support from peers, supervisors and managers was emphasised for workers and teams where a risk-taking approach was being developed. This was identified as particularly important 'where complex risks are involved' and 'especially when things go wrong'.

Difficulties in involving users

A small number of staff reported no difficulties in attempting to get users involved in risk decision making. The features which were identified as helpful here included the presence of multidisciplinary discussion with users, the clear recording of decisions, and taking into account the relevant guidance and legislation. The majority of respondents, nevertheless, pinpointed a range of problems. These can be grouped as follows.

The first group of problems involved communication difficulties, for example in not being able to explain risk taking well enough to clients. Involvement was found to be very difficult where users have profound mental and physical disabilities, with little or no verbal communication, and there were issues raised by staff acting as advocates for risk. One informant noted that it depends on capacity relative to the stages of risk management; another, gloomily, that it was difficult to support people in choices which were likely to fail. Others pointed to factors such as possible difficulties with management; developing methods of common understanding of processes used in assessment; and difficulties in reaching consensus.

Conflict with carers and parents, such as in those instances involving 'relatives disputing risk decisions', formed the second set of difficulties. Negative attitudes held by carers could act as a major stumbling block for client and staff. A third group consisted of the difficulties entailed in negotiating acceptable risk. Continuing support was seen by some respondents as necessary for people to accept decisions and the consequences; it would also help overcome problems caused by fear, lack of knowledge, disempowerment and unrealistic expectations. The fourth and final group of difficulties revolved around problems with public perceptions, where the risks of harmful or dangerous occurrences were often wildly exaggerated, making it sometimes difficult to engage constructively with local communities. This theme often appeared in training sessions and provided much scope for discussion and debate.

Key skills for confident risk takers

In this section we outline and consider some of the key skills which professionals, other carers and vulnerable individuals need to develop to allow them to become more confident and skilled risk takers. The gaps in the literature have already been commented upon many times in this book, so it will come as no surprise to the reader that there is little about the kinds of skills which health and social work professionals require in relation to risk taking and even less about the skills which their clients need. This section represents a preliminary examination of an area which is evidently ripe for further exploration.

What kinds of skills are needed for confident risk taking? Let us start with professionals and their skills. There is evidence from the training courses run by the author and from the research conducted for Titterton (1999): here professionals identified the kinds of skills which they perceived as important for risk taking. A range of skills is encompassed within these perceptions as it will become clear below. Other studies, such as that by Gorman (2003) of care managers, have found decision making and risk management are considered professional activities that demand the acquisition and development of specific skills.

Stanley and Manthorpe have drawn attention to the chorus of demands for training. The problem is that training by itself is simply perceived as the solution to problems, yet these problems sometimes have roots in policy and resource issues which lie beyond the sphere of professional practice. A critique of this is presented in Titterton (1999) which points up the limitations of training in risk work. How can we train professionals and others in the art of making 'judgement calls'? The role of decision making in risk asessment and management is crucial, yet we have only started to scratch the surface in terms of exploring this particular issue. What are the competences which underpin the making of risk decisions? How can they be evidenced?

A key difficulty is with the knowledge base: as Kelly (1996, p.114) notes, there is a 'lack of a generally accepted theoretical framework for the facts and knowledge its assessment processes generate'. Without these frameworks, he suggests, it is hard to interpret facts and use knowledge in a consistent way – and so workers tend to fall back on 'common sense' use of accumulated practice. He cites evidence from the literature to support his assertion. We can also point here to the findings of studies such as Benbenishty *et al.* (2003) and Gale *et al.* (2002, 2003) about the sorts of knowledge social workers and mental health workers use when assessing risks, mentioned in Chapter 3. Studies of different kinds of knowledge by practitioners of risk and illness were also cited there, such as Clarke (2000); Gilmour *et al.* (2003); Kemshall (2000); see also Adams' (2001) account of the construction of risk by community psychiatric nurses and informal carers of those with dementia.

However, Kelly goes on to propose that social services and social workers have a particular responsibility to develop and use frameworks, especially for child abuse, and especially those that have potential for providing a base for rational decision making. There is plenty of material, he suggests finally, in the field of child abuse. The difficulty here is that while he is right in the sense that there is a lot of material, it is hard to see how it adds up to any coherent framework. This is particularly so for the field of vulnerable adults.

Some workers are unsure about the skills needed and look for guidance from the trainer. However, they often have a great deal of experience and many will have been using the kinds of skills required without consciously recognising it. These skills include creative skills; creativity is important but is is often stifled by bureaucracies lacking in imagination in management and policies.

Three sets of skills which should be seen as essential to developing good practice in risk work are discussed below.

Interprofessional working

Increasingly, interprofessional working is becoming more important for health and social welfare practitioners (see e.g. Leathard 2003; Ovretveit *et al.* 1997; Walker 2003) and this is reflected in the growing interest in interprofessional education (Tucker 2003). Beresford and Trevillion (1995) outline a number of skills for collaboration in community care plainly relevant in the context of multiagency working in risk work which are:

- communication
- using appropriate language, style of communication
- relationship work including handling conflict, confronting discrimination, developing trust, developing support
- empowerment including advocacy, involving users and carers in defining and assessing quality, promoting responsiveness
- collaborative working including clarifying goals, roles and tasks
- skills in review and evaluation, including self-criticism.

Beresford and Trevillion talk of the 'skills profile' for collaborating, which they see as a way for 'transforming welfare'. Other writers, such as Landau (2000), have noted that resolving ethical dilemmas often involves an inter-disciplinary process and so professionals need to consider improving their communication skills. 'Partnership working' is highlighted by both the Scottish and English documents on the training of social workers (Scottish Executive 2003; Department of Health 2002) and is now perceived as the way forward for developing empowering relationships (McWilliam and Coleman 2003). This is the case for those working both in the statutory sector and in the voluntary sector, though it is no magic solution and important issues remain for policymakers and practitioners to address (Titterton *et al.* 2000).

Negotiation

A core skill for professionals (and lay persons) is that of negotiation. The Manchester Open Learning Project describes 'negotiation' as 'going about your business and pursuing your interests in a way which interacts with the work and interests of others' (1993, p.83). People do it all the time without even thinking about it. Negotiation takes place every time the interests of one person or group are dependent on the action of another person or group who also have interests to pursue; and those respective interests are pursued by cooperative means.

Bibby (1994) refers to the idea of 'assertive negotiation'. This is a useful term because it involves us standing up for ourselves but in a way which respects the rights of others. Here are some helpful guidelines on negotiation derived from Bibby and the Manchester Open Learning Project.

- Ideal preferences should be stated.
- Do not negotiate the unnegotiable.
- Do not negotiate over positions.
- Prepare for give and take but know your boundaries.
- Know what you are trying to achieve.
- Separate people from the problem.
- Look at your interests and other people's interests.
- Be prepared to fail to agree.

Facilitation

Another essential skill for risk work is that of facilitation. Bentley has criticised definitions of facilitation for failing to mention what he rightly sees as the key aspect of facilitation, namely the empowerment of individuals. He suggests this definition: 'facilitation is about empowering people to take control and responsiblity for their own efforts and achievements' (1994, p.28). This definition helps to capture the notion of encouraging vulnerable people to have more say over their lives but also to assume responsiblity for their decisions in relation to risk. The aim of facilitation in this sense is to encourage and give people increasing responsibility for taking control. For Bentley, this involves 'the provision of opportunities, resources, encouragement and support' for groups to succeed in achieving their objectives (1994, p.28)

However as Pont (1996) points out, facilitation requires more skills beyond those employed by the traditional trainer. He suggests the good facilitator is one who is:

- sensitive to people and situations
- perceptive
- tolerant
- patient
- empathetic
- open, candid and trusting.

The need now is for facilitation skills to be developed, not just in trainers, but in welfare professionals and in laypersons too, including users if possible.

Skills for lay people

The term 'lay persons' in this context refers to people who are not welfare professionals or policy makers and includes users of health and social services, as well as informal carers. Often little in the way of training is provided to such groups, especially in terms of risk taking. A range of skills was identified in the author's research described above. The key skills include:

- gaining insight
- communication
- reflection
- learning

- negotiation
- assertiveness
- managing stress
- compromising.

The skills are basically the same as for welfare practitioners, though different emphases for certain topics such as assertiveness may be appropriate. The skills described above, such as negotiation, are also highly relevant for lay persons and will help them to better secure the services they want for themselves or for other people, such as family members. Other basic but necessary skills are sometimes clustered under the term 'lifeskills' (see e.g. Hopson and Scally 1980, 1982, 1986) or 'problem solving skills' (see e.g. Priestley *et al.* 1978).

Working with vulnerable people involves working closely with the people and/or their advocates in getting the people themselves to identify their needs and wants and to work through what is involved in taking a decision about risk. For example, a person can be helped to identify key supports, how he or she copes with life and taking risks (aspects of this approach have been used in the Assist Toolkit which the author worked on; see Assist (Scotland) 1998). Moreover, training can be provided to help service users and informal carers participate more effectively in their own risk assessments, as was mentioned in Chapter 5.

The empowerment of service users and carers is supposed to be high on the agenda of welfare providers (see for example Bettesworth *et al.* 2003; Byrt and Dooher 2003; Jackson and Hyslop 2003). Examples include the growth of lay assessment of service plans and service provision, though these are sometimes criticised as tokenistic (Belcher *et al.* 2003). Some attempts have been made to involve people with disabilities in a course to work in partnership with professionals and service providers (Lordan 2000), as well as to involve users in social work training (Beresford 2003), in assessing students on practice placements (Edwards 2003) and in training for mental health staff (Bettesworth *et al.* 2003). The Department of Health (2002) has also made explicit a desire to see users involved in the selection of social work students, as well as in other aspects of social work education.

It is nevertheless difficult to see genuine empowerment happening without more widespread and sustained support and training for users and carers, particularly in the field of risk work. A bottom-up approach to empower front-line professionals, service users and informal carers through skills development, training and other forms of support would represent a very worthwhile investment.

Reflective practice

The question of how practitioners can best learn risk assessment and management skills has to be addressed by managers, trainers and educationalists alike. Practitioners learn from each other and from working with other professions, and they require more learning opportunities involving imaginative formats and stimulation through a variety of training methods. A judicious mixture of theory and practice is essential; the need for supervision must also be acknowledged (Burke 1997). Both the Department of Health (2002) and the Scottish Executive (2003) have emphasised the need for practice-based learning to enhance the training and education of social workers. Risk taking is not an area which can be learned theoretically; experiential learning is best. Reflection is a critical skill for risk takers, as captured by the notion of the 'reflective practitioner' (Gould and Taylor 1996; Schon 1983).

The growth of 'reflective practice' in health and social care is a welcome development (Burns and Bulman 2000). This represents an attempt to help practitioners develop as better professionals through critically reflecting on their practice, reviewing useful learning points which they can draw out of a situation. The idea that the development of risk assessment and management skills should be part of a gradual and reflective learning process has to be emphasised. A system such as PRAMS is intended to encourage people who use it to focus more sharply on skills development and to review constantly what they have learned.

The limits of what training and trainers can achieve should, nevertheless, be borne in mind; more realistic expectations are required. Training, it has to be said, provides the start, not the end, of this process. What would be particularly welcome are further research studies of how practitioners learn and develop risk-taking skills, and what contribution trainers can make. Such studies would make a most useful contribution to the literature relating to research and training (Titterton 1999).

Conclusion

In this chapter issues for the training of professionals and lay persons in risk taking have been reviewed. An attempt was made to fill in some of the gaps in the literature. Attention was drawn to the numerous calls for training but it has also been argued that training is a starting point, not a solution to the sort of problems which are often cited in government and other reports. There is an urgent need to find out more about appropriate training methodologies in risk work; one evaluated approach, the PRAMS model, was discussed in terms of research findings from participants. In particular, there is a necessity to test the effectiveness of training in relation to different kinds of professionals. Training which is multidisciplinary and multiagency in nature can be particularly beneficial. A better understanding of the learning process and development of risk competences is required and more realistic perceptions of training and its context are needed.

Research has been cited that pinpoints the sorts of skills that professionals have identified as important and guidelines put forward for working with professionals and with vulnerable people in the area of making risk decisions. Greater emphasis will have to be placed on the training of both welfare professionals and laypeople if risk taking is to be made to work, with a more significant investment of resources. Empowerment for service users and informal carers is unlikely to happen without more serious efforts made to involve them in training, both to educate professionals and to develop skills in their own right.

Conclusion

The preceding chapters of this book have, in the discussion of risk and risk taking, emphasised the potential for creativity and imagination among welfare professionals, their managers, and the users of services, their informal carers and the communities they live in. Thus the 'professional imagination' can be developed and set free in ways which will help liberate people from the confines of their disability and which will facilitate their choices in a life-enhancing fashion.

The research undertaken for this book has found that professionals are more willing to experiment with innovative styles of working with vulnerable people than perhaps has been previously realised within the literature. This creativity arising from attempts to resolve welfare dilemmas – defined earlier as addressing the choices that welfare practitioners, vulnerable people and their informal carers face between options which entail possible benefits and possible harms – is a cause for celebration for hard-pressed professions accustomed to finding themselves in the harsh glare of media attention.

The tendency to conceive of risk solely in terms of its negative consequences has been criticised here and a more positive understanding of risk and risk taking has been put forward. The current limitations of the literature(s) in this field have been reviewed and discussed. However, the research also shows that professionals are experimenting with new understandings of risk and managers are starting to work with new frameworks and are taking steps to develop risk policies for their agencies.

That there is a long way to go, in setting those frameworks, in capturing their spirit in workable policies, and in putting these into practice remains the case. The research has found that there were few worked-up examples of such policies, many were still very much in draft stages and some lagged some way behind practice on the ground. It was also found that assessment received an undue emphasis, often being concentrated upon at the expense of the policy framework. Too much work was being put into assessment forms and not enough into systematically surveying fundamental principles and working these up into sound operational policies. Risk management was also found to be underdeveloped in relation to risk assessment within agencies and departments.

The discussion in this book has stressed the importance of logically setting out the main stages for risk taking: underlying principles and values, policies, key steps for assessment, key steps for risk management; and linking these together into one coherent process. Assessments need to be clearly tied into key principles and policies and then integrated with the risk management process. How this can be done has been demonstrated through the use of the Person-centred Risk Assessment and Management System model.

This model, as its name suggests, is sharply focused on the vulnerable individual and his or her needs and interests. The aim is to facilitate and enhance the choices and opportunities of the individual, to open new windows in the person's life. At the same time, the model is intended to provide the practitioner and his or her agency with a coherent set of checks and balances, which respect their rights, as well as the rights of the vulnerable person.

It is this balancing of rights and choices, in weighing up welfare dilemmas and in negotiating compromises, that lies at the heart of the professional enterprise in the field of risk taking. Risk taking, as we have seen, is purposive action based on informed decisions concerning both good and bad outcomes in relation to risks appropriate in certain situations. Uncertainty is fundamental to taking risks and has to be embraced as part of that enterprise.

If community care is to work and if the quality of care in residential and hospital settings is to be improved, then risk taking must be recognised as a major issue for practitioners and for service users alike. Even in those areas which appear tightly circumscribed by legislation, media interest and public expectation, such as work with children and work with offenders, there is scope for a more positive reconsideration of how risk is conceived and assessed, as is contended in Appendix 1.

The training described in Chapter 8 showed that there is a great deal of lively interest in the topic by the participants from social work, health and independent sector settings, reflected in their contributions to the training sessions. The participants had many valuable ideas and experiences to contribute to the sessions and to share with each other. The training sessions revealed that there are some difficult and complex dilemmas under the topic of risk taking for which there is no easy resolution. The fine art of professional judgment involved (e.g. in weighing up the balance between risk and safety) was still being developed in both residential and community settings. Four points constantly emerged as key themes in the closing sessions of the training: the necessity for training and development of practitioners and manager; the need for identifying good practice in risk taking; the value of providing appropriate guidance tailored to each care setting; and the importance of managerial support in helping practitioners to make difficult decisions about risks. The PRAMS model was perceived by participants as valuable in setting out a framework for meeting these requirements.

Something approaching a cultural revolution will be needed for policy makers, welfare managers and practitioners to embrace the full implications of the 'risk society' in relation to welfare policy and practice. The current emphasis on the regulation agenda throughout the four countries of the UK was questioned in Chapter 2. Public debate about risk and risk taking, and how scarce resources can best be used, would be welcome. In this respect, the role of the media and those risk communication processes examined by writers such as Bennett and others (see e.g. Bennett 2001; Coles 2001) has to be addressed, something of which welfare practitioners are all too conscious. Efforts to improve the risk communication strategies of those in the front-line should, therefore, be encouraged (see e.g. Edwards *et al.* 1999; French and Maule 2001).

Coote (1998) has argued, in her discussion of risk and trust, that a different kind of relationship is needed between the public and policy makers – a more adult-to-adult relationship with politicians, scientists and 'experts', where the knowledge and experience of each is respected. This will lead to a new kind of public policy making and help generate new understandings. Similarly, a different kind of relationship between service users and service providers, based on a mutual respect of each other's knowledge and experience, will also lead to a more liberating kind of welfare policy and practice. The ramifications of Beck's (1992) analysis of the tension between 'expert and non-expert' risk assessments have yet to be properly explored in relation to debates over risk management in welfare settings, though some authors have rightly drawn attention to the range of 'non-expert' management strategies that can be found, for example, among young drug users (Duff 2003).

In Chapter 8 it was noted that service users and informal carers need more support and training; this is all the more important if 'non-expert' assessments and management strategies are to be given due consideration by policy makers and practitioners. If the empowerment agenda is to get off the ground, then new understandings of risk and risk taking must lie at the heart of the fashioning of new relationships between those in need of welfare services and those charged with meeting those needs.

Key messages from this book

What follows is a summary of some of the key messages emerging from the discussion contained in the preceding chapters.

Policy makers

- Ensure policies facilitate risk-taking approaches.
- Review and develop legislation that is coherent and consistent with human rights and responsibilities.
- Make available sufficient resources to support managers and practitioners.
- Work with the media to encourage better understanding of risk.

Managers

- Develop management frameworks to develop risk taking and ensure assessment and management processes are linked and reviewed.

- Provide support for staff involved in risk taking, including supervisory and counselling processes.
- Ensure staff are adequately trained and confident.
- Ensure resources reach staff at the sharp end of decision making.
- Disseminate the results of good practice.

Practitioners

- Risk-taking approaches can enhance practice and improve outcomes for clients.
- Embrace welfare dilemmas as part of the professional craft.
- Be aware of legislation, rights and responsibilities.
- Work closely with other disciplines and agencies.
- Work in more empowering ways with users and carers.
- Disseminate the results of good practice.

Service users and informal carers

- Taking risks can help improve quality of life.
- Be aware of your rights and be prepared to seek help in ensuring your voice is heard.
- Be aware of your responsibilities – risk taking is shared activity.
- Actively participate in assessing risks and plans to manage risks.
- Press for involvement in training to learn skills for self and to help professionals improve.

Researchers

Many gaps were uncovered in the reviews of the literatures considered throughout this book. The principal lacunae include:

- theoretical development, particularly the articulation of a positive conception of risk and the formulation of middle-range concepts to link 'big theory' with practical concerns

- the potential of risk as a learning process for children and young people
- the interconnections between risk, resilience and protective factors
- research accounts of positive risk assessment
- risk assessments as a learning experience for practitioners and their clients
- risk management based on positive risk taking, including links with assessment processes
- the kinds of skills which health and social work professionals require in relation to risk taking and the skills which their clients need
- involvement of users in lay assessment and management of risks
- training of professionals in risk taking, as well as the participation of users and carers.

Educators

- Learn and pass on the messages from the research community.
- Clearly specify the competences for high quality risk work.
- Identify and agree the key skills required for high quality risk work.
- Spell out the implications for learning structures and processes.
- Develop more learning opportunities in practice settings and work places.

Assessing Risk of Serious Harm in Health and Social Care Settings: The Examples of Child Protection and Sex Offenders

'Risk' in the context of welfare work with children and with offenders has become increasingly fraught for practitioners and managers, owing to mounting concerns expressed by the media, politicians and sections of the public in the wake of high publicity cases in the UK. Working with these groups represents a prime example of the 'politics of risk communication' mentioned earlier in this book. This has had unfortunate consequences for the conceptualisation and assessment of risk by health and welfare professionals in these particular fields.

A principal concern in areas such as child abuse, mental health work and criminal justice is what Kemshall has called the 'quest for prediction', or in other words, the 'art of foretelling that an event, behaviour or action will occur' (Kemshall 1996, p.134). Before this quest is embarked upon, however, we should be clear about why we are doing this and what we hope to achieve. The point was raised in Chapter 5, as made by Sargent (1999), to the effect that child protection aimed at the detection and prevention of abuse and harm is looking through too narrow a frame. Complexities such as child and family relationships, it was suggested, are overlooked. A similar argument can be made in respect in offenders, where the minimisation of harm and danger has become an overriding preoccupation.

It can be contended that the search for accurate prediction is often misplaced and that instead we should be using the concept of 'risk' to think again about our basic assumptions and grasp the exciting opportunities it affords for professional practice and for vulnerable individuals and their carers. We also need to clarify our language, to talk not of 'children at risk' but rather of 'children at risk of harm'.

Definitional issues

Risk work with children and with offenders poses particular problems because of the definitional issues that arise:

1.   The definitions of 'child abuse' and 'sexual abuse' are contested.

2.   Shifts have been taking place in key terms, e.g. the move from 'high risk' to 'significant harm' in child protection.

3.   'Risk' is often defined in a negative way, emphasising danger and harm, and positive outcomes or benefits of risk taking are overlooked.

Our understanding of risk has become distorted through preoccupations not just with negative outcomes but also with 'dangerousness' (see also the discussion in Steadman *et al.* 1993; Manthorpe and Stanley 2002; Skeem *et al.* 2004). This is reflected in many definitions of 'risk' and has led to an unbalanced understanding of this concept, which in turn has impacted on professional practice.

The pressures on welfare professionals to go for safety rather than to take risks were mentioned at the start of this book. There are pressures on health and care workers from families, carers and from other professionals, as well as from law makers, the media and the public at large. This is particularly the case in working with children, with offenders and with those with serious mental health problems. Care workers and other professionals come to place an absolute priority on safety; their fear is that they will be seen as bad workers or to have failed in their role if a person is injured or injures himself/herself while under their care. This leads to the attitude that vulnerable people need to be protected from activities which may be dangerous, and leads in turn to an emphasis on the use of restraint and restriction. This becomes caught up in distorted perceptions of risk by the public, fuelled by the media, also mentioned earlier (Bennett and Calman 2001; Franklin 1998). It can, in turn, lead to the infamous cul-de-sac of the 'damned if you do, damned if you don't' dilemma, which so many health and welfare practitioners complain about (e.g. see Davidson-Arad *et al.* 2003).

The legislative framework for child protection

As noted in Chapter 2, no statutory framework for 'risk taking' exists as such. For vulnerable children, there is now a more coherent body of law in the UK than was previously the case, of which the Children Acts of the late 1980s and mid 1990s form key components; new Acts designed to improve the safeguarding of children and their rights are being developed across the four countries of the UK.

In England and Wales, the main legislative planks are:

- Children and Young People Act 1969
- Mental Health Act 1983
- Children Act 1989 – major legislation covering children and their rights
- Data Protection Act 1998
- Human Rights Act 1998 – 2000
- Children (Leaving Care) Act 2000
- Freedom of Information Act 2000
- Criminal Justice and Court Services Act 2000
- Education Act 2002
- Mental Health Bill
- Children Bill – amended in May 2004 and covers establishment of Children's Commissioner; cooperation of services; safeguards and arrangements

to promote welfare; information databases; Local Safeguarding Children's Boards

There is, in addition, a range of other legal measures of relevance throughout the health, social care, housing, education and juvenile justice fields. Other forthcoming legislation of note includes the Domestic Violence, Crime and Victims Bill, some of whose provisions apply throughout the UK, and the Anti-Social Behaviour Bill. A framework for children's issues has been set out by the Government in the Green Paper, *Every Child Matters*, (Department for Education and Skills 2003; Department of Health 2004b); to reflect the 'unprecedented public debate on services for children, young people and families', a document, *Every Child Matters: The Next Steps*, has been issued as a response to the consultation (Department for Education and Skills 2004, p.1).

There is a separate Welsh equivalent entitled *Children and Young People: Rights to Action* (Welsh Assembly 2004). Wales was the first country to set up a children's commissioner in 2001, followed by Northern Ireland in 2003 and Scotland in 2004. Provision for a commissioner for England is made in the new Children Bill.

Statutory instruments for Scotland and Wales, as well as provisions made by the Scottish Parliament and Welsh Assembly have added to this body of law. Scotland provides an interesting example because it has so often been innovative in children's services, such as the Children's Hearings System, which has been reviewed of late (Scottish Executive 2004a) and has been pressing ahead with a Children's Charter and Framework for Standards (Scottish Executive 2004e; see also Scottish Executive 2004f). The Children (Scotland) Act 1995 remains an important legislative step, based on similar measures in England, Wales and Northern Ireland.

The principal Acts that impinge on the protection of children include the following measures:

- Social Work (Scotland) Act 1968 – empowers the local authority to promote the welfare of children
- NHS (Scotland) Act 1978 – puts a duty on ministers to provide comprehensive health services and on health boards and local authorities to cooperate
- Education (Scotland) Act 1980
- Housing (Scotland) Act 1987 – duty on local authority to re-house children in homeless families
- Data Protection Act 1984
- Foster Children (Scotland) Act 1984
- Age of Legal Capacity Act 1991
- Children (Scotland) Act 1995 – the main legislation covering children
- Police (Scotland) Act 1997
- Human Rights Act 1998 – 2000
- Freedom of Information Act 2000
- Protection of Children (Scotland) Act 2003 – covers prevention of unsuitable people to work with children

- Commissioner for Children and Young People (Scotland) Act 2003
- Additional Support for Learning Bill – to support children with learning support needs, currently before the Scottish Parliament
- Antisocial Behaviour etc. (Scotland) Bill – passed by the Scottish Parliament in June 2004

This adds up to a wide array of legislative measures for practitioners and others to deal with.

In addition to the development of the Children's Charter and Framework for Standards, there are plans for the multiagency inspection of children's services, starting with child protection in December 2004. The emphasis is on multidisciplinary and multiagency work, as reflected in the example of the Child Protection Committees. A Child Protection Action Team has been taking a lead on these issues within the Scottish Executive.

The Children (Scotland) Act 1995 introduced four new provisions aimed at protecting children from harm or at establishing whether children may be in need of protection from harm: the child assessment order, the child protection order, the exclusion order and emergency child protection measures. Local authorities may apply to use any of the provisions. This reflects their central position in safeguarding and promoting the welfare of children in need. Child protection should, however, be seen in the context of local authorities' wider responsibilities for child care. To assist authorities in discharging those responsibilities, the Act introduces various powers enabling authorities to provide a range of different types of support for children and their families. The effective use of those powers will help to avoid situations which could lead to children being subjected to abuse and may thus avert the need for child protection intervention.

All four provisions require the condition of significant harm to be satisfied. The term 'significant harm' is not defined in the Act. It remains, therefore, a matter for the judgement of those concerned with determining the outcome of applications to consider whether the degree of harm to which the child is believed to have been subjected or is suspected of having been subjected (or is likely to be subjected) is significant.

Risk assessment in work with children at risk of harm

The problems arising from definitional issues are compounded in the area of child protection work, as Corby (1996) notes, by the difficulties in agreeing on the level of seriousness that should be a matter for public concern. In the UK, the state has traditionally been ambivalent about setting the limits of intervention into the private sphere of families and this has led to changes in approaches and reversals in policy (Corby 1996; Parton *et al.* 1997).

Two interrelated problems arise here: the tendency towards the 'over protection' of children and an overwhelming concern about blame – the prevalence of a 'blame culture'.

Not only are definitions of 'risk' often contested, as was noted earlier, but loaded terms such as 'child abuse' remain open to dispute. As Gough (1993) argues, this is no mere definitional argument as it affects the preventive actions we propose to take. 'Child abuse' is a social concept, but one with a political dimension, a point made by an increasing number of writers (e.g. Parton *et al.* 1997).

It is evident that a reconsideration of how professionals conceive issues to do with child abuse and child protection has been taking place within the UK, particularly following cases that have emerged in the last two decades. This is evident in national reviews, such as the National Commission of Inquiry into the Prevention of Child Abuse and its report, *Childhood Matters* (2004). Scotland once again provides a valuable illustration because of the wide-ranging nature of the reviews that have been taking place (see also Daniel 2004). This willingness to broaden the scope of this reconsideration is reflected in the report *It's Everybody's Job To Make Sure I'm Alright* (Scottish Executive 2002), based on consultation with those working in the field and with young people as well. The reviewers sought to bring all the pieces of the jigsaw together to see the complete picture of children's lives and needs. While a number of agencies have specific responsibilities towards children it is the responsibility of all adults to protect children, hence the title, which is a quote from one of the young people who participated in the consultation.

The review found that there is no single agreed definition of what child abuse and neglect is and that definitions have changed over time. Abuse can be physical, sexual or emotional. It may be acute or involve a long-term pattern of physical neglect. Often children are abused in more than one way. As understanding of child abuse and neglect has increased, situations which are considered to be abusive or neglectful have broadened to include:

- organised abuse, for example, children involved in prostitution and ritual abuse
- Munchausen's syndrome by proxy/fabrication or induction of illness in a child by a carer
- foetal abuse, for example through maternal abuse of alcohol or drugs
- domestic abuse (primarily of mothers) which causes physical or emotional abuse of children
- children affected by parental drug abuse
- racial abuse
- female genital mutilation (circumcision)
- forced marriage
- children who need protecting from harming themselves, through self-inflicted injuries or reckless behaviour.

The reviewers also pointed out that over the last twenty years it has emerged that the agencies and individuals with responsibility for children do not always protect them. There is now greater awareness of institutional abuse, for example, physical, emotional or sexual abuse in care homes or schools. More recently, it is claimed, 'system abuse' has been identified where the child protection or criminal justice systems or practices are experienced by children as being abusive.

Children and young people may not always define child abuse and neglect in terms used by official agencies, according to the report. They tend to view child abuse primarily in terms of physical abuse and sexual abuse and are less likely to talk about physical neglect or emotional abuse. Research has shown that some children and young people experiencing abuse may not define it as such because they have learned to regard it as normal or deserved. Peer abuse has been identified as a major worry for children and young people, but according to the reviewers, bullying is not normally defined as child abuse by professionals. Since the report was published however, bullying has become a topic that is increasingly seen as important and there may have to be a re-examination of this issue in the near future.

It was also noted that for many people the term child protection relates to the activities of agencies such as the police and social work services in their protection of individual children. The study of public views in the review suggested that this is the most common understanding. For others, it encompasses a wider range of activities such as making roads safer for children to cross, or educating children about drugs and other harmful substances. While the review examined closely those agencies involved in protecting individual children, a broader approach was taken as to understanding how children might be protected, including through the use of preventive measures.

The Scottish review, however, stopped short of a reconsideration of 'risk' and what this might mean for risk assessment. Recommendations were made in relation to assessment by professionals, which will be mentioned below. It was pointed out that the latter were sometimes more hindered than helped by agency procedures and guidelines. As Kelly (1996) noted, most texts in child abuse and most agency procedures contain lists of 'risk factors' or 'predisposing factors' that can be said to be associated with parenting or caring which is abusive. However such lists are 'fraught with difficulty' (p.115) as they are based on research that is drawn exclusively from groups who have actually abused their children and not from the population as a whole. In the field of physical abuse, the checklist approach has also been applied to long-term assessments. Greenland (1987), in the wake of the Beckford inquiry, drew up a checklist of factors associated with 100 child death cases investigated in Canada and Great Britain. Typically such lists include both child and parental factors, with examples of the latter being prior histories of abuse and social isolation. However the predictive value of many of the factors may be limited, as Corby (1996) has pointed out. Thompson (1998) is also among those who question the reliance on the checklist approach.

Corby (1996) also argues that social workers in Britain have not till recently explicitly used rational methods of assessing risks. In respect of physical abuse and neglect cases, Corby and Mills (1986) found a range of factors to be implicitly influencing conference decisions, including parent-related factors such as parental character and cooperation. Waterhouse and Carnie (1992) found a slightly different set of factors operating in sexual abuse cases, though these also included parental attitude to the investigation. Corby and Mills (1986) have contended that there is need to make the use of criteria such as these explicit, and that professionals need to check through these factors in a systematic way as an aid to deciding on the level of risk at the initial assessment stage. More recently, Little *et al.* (2004) have noted how individual interpretations can alter 'objective' assessments of risk.

In order to meet the shortcomings identified in the Scottish review, the report recommended developing linked computer-based information systems which should include a single integrated assessment, planning and review report framework for children in need (Scottish Executive 2002). For those in need of protection the framework should include reason for concern, needs of the children, plans to meet them and protect them when necessary, and progress since any previous meetings. This core assessment, planning and review framework should be accessible and common to all partner agencies, multiagency case conferences and the children's hearing. Arrangements should be made for appropriate access to information by agencies in other areas should children or their families move.

The review also noted, rightly, that practitioners must account for their evidence gathering and approach to assessment but also for the underlying reasoning behind conclusions that are reached. This requires a level of knowledge and understanding that is not currently in place. Among other recommendations the review stressed that there is a strong need for methods of diagnosis and assessment that are validated; improved evidence gathering and recording; clear plans that directly address identified needs and risks; mechanisms for monitoring of progress and outcomes and identified thresholds for taking protective action.

Now that the inquiries into the cases of Victoria Climbié, Caleb Ness and other recent tragedies have placed risk high on the welfare agenda, it is essential that lessons are learned and that the extensive literature is carefully reviewed, synthesised and disseminated in ways which will impact on professional practice. It is also imperative that narrow and negative constructions of assessment and management are not allowed to dominate. As argued in Chapter 5, developmental perspectives that acknowledge the centrality of risk offer particularly valuable ways of moving forward in this complex area. Some of the difficulties in developing structured risk assessments were also discussed in that chapter. An important consideration is that the rationale behind the assessment must not be lost sight of, nor the focus on the child in terms of his or her welfare. This should remain the case even if broader, 'ecological' frameworks of decision making (Tomison 1999) are adopted.

The legislative framework for sex offenders

The legislative picture for the UK has been changing significantly in recent years. For example, the provisions of the Criminal Justice and Court Services Act 2000 and Sex Offenders Act 2003 profoundly affect arrangements for notification and registration of sex offenders and arrangements for management by local statutory bodies in the community. Again Scotland provides a useful example. The Sex Offenders Act 1997, which governed the registration of offenders, has been repealed and is now consolidated with improvements by Part 2 of the Sex Offence Act 2003 (Part 1 of this Act does not affect Scotland). This includes the provision of Sexual Offences Prevention Orders, which in Scotland can only be made by the Chief Constable. There is however a proposal to extend these orders so that they can be made by the courts. Consideration is also currently being given to the possible introduction of Risk of Sexual Harm measures, to help extend the range of measures available to the authorities.

The Expert Panel on Sex Offending, chaired by Lady Cosgrove, was set up to address the issues raised in the 1997 report *A Commitment to Protect* (Scottish Office 1997a). The MacLean White Paper was published in 2000, with the remit to make proposals for the sentencing and future management and treatment of serious sexual and violent offenders who may pose a continuing risk to the public (MacLean Committee 2000). The recommendations have since been proposed in the Criminal Justice (Scotland) Act which was scrutinised and passed by the Scottish Parliament.

The Criminal Justice (Scotland) Act 2003 included the introduction of a new sentence, the Order for Lifelong Restriction, for the lifetime control of any offender considered by the courts to present a risk and contained provisions to establish a Risk Management Authority to help agencies responsible for offenders. Under the Act the authority will collect information, sponsor research, promulgate best practice, set standards, and accredit risk assessment tools and techniques in the risk management of offenders. It will also have a role in overseeing the implementation and monitoring of Risk Management Plans for the small number of high-risk violent and sexual offenders who have been given the new Order for Lifelong Restriction sentence.

As elsewhere in the UK, local authorities in Scotland have statutory responsibilities for supervising those convicted offenders who are subject to community-based sentences, such as probation, or who are subject to statutory supervision on release from prison. This will include certain sex offenders. They also have a statutory responsibility to provide advice, guidance and assistance to people who, within twelve months of release from custody, ask for this.

Risk assessment in work with sex offenders

As research undertaken for *A Commitment To Protect* (Scottish Office 1997a) shows, sex offenders who abuse children are the most studied group in the research literature (see e.g. Abel and Rouleau 1990; Barker and Morgan 1993; Howard League 1985; Murphy, Haynes and Worley 1991; Thornton 1992; Waterhouse, Dobash and Carnie 1994; Williams and Finkelhor 1991). More recently, young people who sexually abuse others have received greater attention from researchers (see for example Green and Masson 2002).

However, issues and problems in risk assessment work with sex offenders are similar to those encountered in risk assessment of children at risk of harm, with limited understandings of risk, where the focus is often solely on preventing or at least reducing the likelihood of adverse outcomes. Risk assessment in this field is, as *A Commitment To Protect* (Scottish Office 1997a) noted, complex and uncertain. Assessments were found by reviewers to be frequently informal, not recorded and based on professional judgements without necessarily using research findings or the most helpful tools available.

A Commitment To Protect rightly argued that risk assessment remains an imperfect science and that no one model provides all the answers. Assessments should be based, it was suggested, on factors known for their predictive quality. For example, one study (Hanson and Bussière 1996) identified a number of factors that seemed of significance in identifying sex offenders at highest risk of committing a further offence. This should be linked with an assessment of the individual's motivation, circumstances and problems that might impact on any plans to reduce the risk: the likelihood of re-offending, the potential seriousness of any future offending and an assessment of what factors in the offender's social and personal circumstances need to be addressed to reduce the risk (Scottish Office 1997a).

As in work with vulnerable children, checklists have been devised to help practitioners assess the risk of serious harm. Tools intended to measure the risk of re-offending have been developed, based on key indicators of recidivism (see e.g. Barbaree *et al.* 2001; Campbell 2003; Cooke 2000; Corrado *et al.* 2003; Kemshall 2002a; Loucks 2002; McIvor, Kemshall and Levy 2002; Roberts *et al.* 2002). While they can provide a framework for a more structured consideration about the risks an offender poses and the work that should be undertaken to reduce these risks, similar caveats as for the area of children's work must apply in their use.

Best practice, according to the Scottish Office document (1997a), will combine the insights of different disciplines and knowledge of research findings, with careful consideration of the individual offender and information about him or her. To this and to the above discussion about assessment we can add that individual coping strategies and the self management of risk, where the latter is understood in terms of its positive as well as negative connotations, need to be brought into the equation. More attention should be paid by the research community and by practitioners alike to the potential for working with offenders on understanding and addressing risk behaviours (Titterton 2002).

The literature review and the consultation undertaken by the Scottish Office highlighted the difficulties of risk assessment and confirmed that there is no single 'correct' approach. Calls were made for a more coordinated and ordered approach to assist the development of better assessments and it is hoped that the developing expertise in specialist prison and hospital services will contribute to the further development of risk assessment in community monitoring and supervision. An interagency approach to risk assessment was recommended as having considerable merits, particularly for 'high risk' offenders. This is something that the recently formed Public Protection Teams will wish to make a priority in order to make their work more effective.

Towards systematic risk assessment in work with children and sex offenders

Five key points may be made by way of conclusion:

- As long as reasonable safeguards are provided, risk taking provides valuable learning opportunities for all concerned in work with children and work with sex offenders.

- It is important to be systematic in our approach to the assessment of abuse and harm.

- A framework is important for the criteria of day-to-day decisions of experienced practitioners (Waterhouse and Carnie 1992).

- It is essential to secure greater consistency in risk assessment and the evaluation of methods should be given priority.

- Training and agency support for those making risk assessments is crucial.

Special attention, as indicated in Chapter 8, needs to be paid to developing those skills needed to undertake a comprehensive risk assessment, particularly in the context of multidisciplinary and interagency work.

Risk Assessment and Management Plan (Example)

Name of individual: _____

Name of key worker: _____   Date: _____

1. What is the nature of the proposed risk activity? _____

2. What are the reasons for proposing this risk activity? _____

3. Where will the risk activity occur? _____

4. What is the timescale for the risk activity? _____

5. What are the potential benefits?

Please note the main benefits for (a) to (d) and rate each for importance and likelihood.

	Importance rating		Likelihood rating
	For individual	For key worker	
(a) the individual			
(b) family and friends			
(c) other people			
(d) the service/agency			

Importance rating: 1 = not important, 2 = moderately important, 3 = important
Likelihood rating: 1 = unlikely, 2 = may happen, 3 = very likely

6. What are the potential harms?

Please note the main harms for (a) to (d) and rate each for importance and likelihood.

	Importance rating		Likelihood rating
	For individual	For key worker	
(a) the individual			
(b) family and friends			
(c) other people			
(d) the service/agency			

Importance rating: 1 = not important, 2 = moderately important, 3 = important
Likelihood rating: 1 = unlikely, 2 = may happen, 3 = very likely

7. What steps will be taken to minimise possible harms?

8. What steps will be taken to maximise possible benefits?

9. If required, when will intervention take place and how will this happen?

10. What measures of success or failure have been agreed?

11. Who has been consulted?

12. Who is responsible for implementing and reviewing the risk plan?

13. What arrangements will be put in place for monitoring and reviewing?

14. What are the support or training needs, in relation to risk:

(a) of the individual:

(b) of the staff:

15. Any other comments?

Signatures   **Date**

Individual _____ _____

Carer/relative _____ _____

Key worker _____ _____

Manager/Project leader _____ _____

Sample Case Studies

These are some sample case studies used by the author in training exercises, typically using small group methods. The feedback sessions were used as an opportunity to further explore welfare dilemmas and tease out implications of risk decisions for the individual concerned, for families and other informal carers, for practitioners and colleagues, for managers and the agencies involved and for the community.

Questions were posed by the trainer for participants to think about in respect of each case study and to discuss with their partners in small groups.

Case study 1

Bill Hamilton, a retired fisherman, lives with his wife Jessie in a small town. Bill is 74 and has an industrial injury to his back which is now severely restricting his activities. He has impaired vision and a prostate problem. He has always been fiercely proud of his independence but increasingly needs help with self-care tasks and with getting around the house. Jessie is 69, small in stature, and often finds it difficult to cope with the physical demands of a husband who weighs 14 stone. Till recently she has never seen her husband entirely naked and she is struggling to cope with the growing necessity of caring for her husband on the one hand and respecting his desire for privacy and independence on the other. She has become depressed, worn out physically and emotionally and has become isolated from her circle of friends.

The Hamiltons live in a first-floor flat which they own. Their accommodation is often cold in winter months and it is in a state of poor repair. Their one surviving son, on a recent visit from Australia, suggested to his parents that they should consider moving to a nearby residential home. Bill, however, is reluctant to move and is equally reluctant to get help in.

Questions

1. Discuss the needs of Bill and Jessie.
2. How can the quality of life of the couple be improved?
3. What choices do those involved have?
4. How can the respective needs and rights of the couple be balanced?

Case study 2

Flossie Isbister is 82 and has for the last 15 years lived with her daughter Rosemary on an island off the mainland of Britain. She is now suffering from a progressive and rapid deterioration due to the onset of Alzheimer's disease. Rosemary is 58 and is contemplating her retirement from a part-time job with a small firm. She is worried about the apparent rapid decline in Flossie's faculties and particularly her memory. Flossie has begun to leave pots burning on the stove and to develop some forms of obsessive behaviour. She often berates her daughter for not finding favourite clothes (e.g. a cardigan) which she stopped wearing many years before. She keeps trying to phone old friends and neighbours, then forgetting she has called and ringing them again. They have asked Rosemary to see if she can stop her mother doing this if she can. Over the last year Flossie has worsened considerably. Rosemary is becoming very overworked and stressed from the demands of her job and the demands of looking after her mother. Her mother has taken increasingly to night-time wandering. Flossie's GP has commented on this and has suggested either a nursing home or some form of long-term care as a possible solution.

In the course of her wandering Flossie fell and suffered a severely fractured hip. She has been in hospital now for two months. She is presently under observation in an assessment ward of the local hospital which currently has long-term wards available. Flossie seems disorientated and can be aggressive towards staff and other patients in her ward, particularly if they attempt to stop her attempts at wandering during the day.

Rosemary is uncertain about what she should do for her mother. She does not feel she can cope with her in the house any longer, at least on her own. She is also concerned about the relatively remote circumstances of the island where their house is.

Questions

1.   What are the different needs of Flossie and Rosemary?

2.   What are the choices they face?

3.   What are the limits of acceptable risk for both of them?

4.   What about Flossie's wandering? Does it matter? Can it be managed?

Case study 3

Alice McDonald is a young woman aged 21 who has moderate learning disabilities and some physical impairment. She had lived with her parents who were very protective of her. Her parents are concerned that she seems to be sexually immature for her age and that she is very amenable and very trusting of people. After much persuasion and discussion with the parents, Alice moved into a group home with six people. However, she complained that people kept asking her to do things for them around the flat and that she did not have any relaxation. She kept expressing an interest in having 'a place of my own'.

After another period of consultation and discussion, Alice finally moved into a small flat which she shares with another young woman from the group home. Alice's support worker remains concerned about her apparent struggle with skills for independence: for example, Alice finds it hard to budget properly. The support worker is often round at the flat checking up on Alice. Her parents also visit her regularly and her mother often does her laundry for her and brings groceries and other household items.

Questions

1.   How would you weigh up the advantages and disadvantages of the situation Alice is now in?

2.   Should Alice be allowed to make her own mistakes?

3.   What advice would you give to the support worker, e.g. on where to draw the limits for intervention?

Case study 4

A young man of 26, William Hood, is diagnosed with schizophrenia and has been an inpatient of Strathpepper Hospital, a mental hospital in a predominantly rural area. He was discharged and went to live with his parents, with whom he stayed prior to admission, but he does not want to stay with them. William wants his own tenancy; however, he is prone to bouts of temper born of frustration and can be very destructive to furniture and fittings when in this state. His previous experience as a tenant of Strathpepper Association for Mental Health was not a happy one, and ended abruptly when he destroyed all the furniture in the Association's flat. His parents have great concerns about his ability to feed himself properly and about his personal hygiene. However William appears adamant that he cannot stay with his parents, other than for short stays, and that he would like to live independently.

Questions

1.   Is William's ambition to have his own tenancy a realistic one?

2.   What is your evaluation of the risks involved for:

    (a)   William

    (b)   those planning his discharge

    (c)   his parents

    (d)   potential landlords?

3.   What steps might be taken to

    (a)   minimise possible harms and

    (b)   increase possible benefits?

Case study 5

Danny is ten years old and after a number of difficult placements with foster parents is now staying in a children's unit. His background includes very poor early parenting and he has a history of severe behavioural problems. Disruption has been a key feature of his life to date. Danny is passionate about football and enjoys games; however, he does not form relationships easily and he gets into fights with staff and other children alike. He can be an exhausting and wearing child and seems to take a delight in pushing boundaries of behaviour to their very limits. Danny is now developing a reputation as a child with aggressive and challenging behaviour.

Questions

1. How would you assess the options and risks in Danny's case?

2. What sort of agreement on acceptable controls is possible for Danny? How might this be accomplished?

Case study 6

Joe McGuire is a 72-year-old man with communication difficulties who lives on his own in an elderly house in need of repair. Joe is fiercely independent and only accepts help and advice reluctantly; however, his increasing arthritic problems are causing him difficulties. He appears very attached to his dog Bobic, a rather temperamental Doberman, the subject of complaint by anxious neighbours. Joe finds it hard to communicate with his neighbours and has retreated into his own world, which includes periodic bouts of alcoholism and depression. His neighbours claim he can be aggressive sometimes, especially when drunk.

The house is often cold and gloomy, as he is reluctant to bum electricity and gas; his main source of heat seems to be a smoky paraffin heater. His carpets are well worn and there are loose stair rods and broken banisters on the stairs. He collects old magazines and newspapers that lie in tottering piles around the house. Various chemicals and substances, including his cleaning fluids, lie around in unmarked jars and lemonade bottles. A much-loved Triumph Bonneville motorcycle lies in many pieces in his kitchen, while tools and spare parts litter the floor and the hall.

Joe hates changes and gets agitated when anyone attempts to tidy up the house or move his things around.

Questions

1. What are the risks for Joe?

2. What are the risks for health and social care staff coming into his home?

3. What are the risks for other people, such as his neighbours?

4. What measures can be taken to work with Joe to:

    (a) minimise the possibility of harm from the hazards in his home?

    (b) increase positive outcomes for Joe?

A Note on Health and Safety Issues

The basis of health and safety law in Britain is provided by the Health and Safety at Work etc Act 1974. This Act sets out the general duties that employers have towards employees and members of the public, and employees have to themselves and to each other. Since the Act was passed, the development of UK health and safety law has been influenced by European law. The Management of Health and Safety at Work Regulations 1992 make more explicit what employers are required to do to manage health and safety under the Act, and they apply to every work activity.

Employers now have placed upon them a requirement to carry out a risk assessment. It should be noted that risk is defined narrowly in terms of negative or harmful outcomes: 'hazard means anything that can cause harm' and 'risk is the chance, high or low, that somebody will be harmed by the hazard'. In addition, employers also need to make arrangements for implementing the health and safety measures identified as necessary by the risk assessment and need to provide clear information and training to employees.

Apart from the Management Regulations, other regulations have been formulated, which make up a body of common provision in health and safety law. These include the following:

- Employers' Liability (Compulsory Insurance) Regulations 1969: require employers to take out insurance against accidents and ill-health to their employees;
- Health and Safety (First Aid) Regulations 1982: cover the requirements for first aid;
- Workplace (Health, Safety and Welfare Regulations 1992: cover a wide range of basic health and safety issues such as lighting, heating and welfare facilities
- Manual Handling Operations Regulations 1992: cover the moving of objects by hand or bodily force
- Personal Protective Equipment (PPE) Regulations 1992: require employers to provide appropriate protective clothing and equipment for employees
- Reporting of Injuries, Diseases and Dangerous Occurrences Regulations1995 (RIDDOR): require employers to notify certain occupational injuries, diseases and dangerous events

- Provision and Use of Work Equipment Regulations (PUWER) 1998: require that equipment provided for use at work is safe
- Control of Substances Hazardous to Health Regulations 1999 (COSHH): require employers to assess the risks from hazardous substances and take precautions.

Often in the health and social services people are in the position of working alone, and increasingly working in the context of other people's domestic environments, as care is provided less in institutional settings and more in community and domestic settings. There is no general legal prohibition on working alone and the broad duties of the Health and Safety Act and the Management of Health and Safety At Work Regulations still apply. Employers still retain responsibilities for the health, safety and welfare at work of their employees and the health and safety of those affected by the work. As the Health and Safety Executive notes, these responsibilities cannot be transferred to people who work alone. The employer still has a duty to assess risks to lone workers and take steps to avoid or control risk (of harm) where necessary. Employees have responsibilities too: they should take reasonable care of themselves and other people affected by their work and cooperate with their employers in meeting the legal obligations.

Employers who employ people who work alone are encouraged to identify all relevant hazards and to take appropriate measures to control such hazards. These measures might include training, supervision, instruction, protective equipment and so on. Employers also need to take steps to check that these measures are used and to review the risk assessment from time to time to make sure that it is still adequate. They also need to be aware of any specific law on lone working that applies to their particular industry.

References

Abel, G.C. and Rouleau, J.L. (1990) 'The nature and extent of sexual assault.' In W.L. Marshall, D.R. Laws and H.E. Barbaree (eds) *Handbook of Sexual Assault*. New York: Plenum.

Adam, B., Beck, U. and Van Loon, J. (2000) *The Risk Society and Beyond: Critical Issues for Social Theory*. London: Sage.

Adams, T. (2001) 'The social construction of risk by community psychiatric nurses and family carers for people with dementia.' *Health, Risk and Society 3*, 3, 307–319.

Aggleton, P. (1996) *Health Promotion and Young People*. London: Health Education Authority.

Alaszewski, A. and Manthorpe, J. (1991) 'Literature review: Measuring and managing risk in social welfare.' *British Journal of Social Work 21*, 277–290.

Alaszewski, A. and Manthorpe, J. (1998) 'Welfare agencies and risk: The missing link.' *Health and Social Care in the Community 6*, 1, 4–15.

Alaszewski, A., Harrison, J. and Manthorpe, J. (1998) *Risk, Health and Welfare*. Buckingham: Open University Press.

Alberg, C., Bingley, W., Bowers, L., Ferguson, G., Hatfield, B., Hoban, A. and Maden, A. (1996) *Learning Materials on Mental Health: Risk Assessment*. University of Manchester Department of Health.

Anglin, J.P. (2002) 'Risk, well being and paramountcy in child protection: The need for transformation.' *Child and Youth Care Forum 31*, 4, 233–255.

Anthony, E.J. (1987) 'Risk, vulnerability and resilience: an overview.' In E.J. Anthony and B.J. Cohler (eds) *The Invulnerable Child*. London: Guilford Press.

Assist (Scotland) (1998) *Assist Toolkit*. Edinburgh: Assist (Scotland).

Argall, P. and Cowderoy, B. (1997) 'We can take it: Young people and drug use.' In H. Kemshall and J. Pritchard (eds) *Good Practice in Risk Assessment and Management*. London: Jessica Kingsley Publishers.

Ayre, P. (1998) 'Asssessment of significant harm: Improving professional practice.' *British Journal of Nursing 7*, 1, 31–36.

Bannister, A. (1998) *From Hearing to Healing: Working with the Aftermath of Child Sexual Abuse*. Chichester and New York: John Wiley.

Barbaree, H.E., Seto, M.C., Langton, C.M. and Peacock, E.J. (2001) 'Evaluating the predictive accuracy of six risk assessment instruments for adult sex offenders.' *Criminal Justice and Behavior 28*, 4, 490–521.

Barker, M. and Morgan, R. (1993) *Sex Offenders: A Framework for the Evaluation of Community-based Treatment*. London: Home Office.

Barker, N.C. and Araji, S. (1998) *Child Abuse and Neglect: An Interdisciplinary Method of Treatment*. Dubuque, IA: Kendall/Hunt Publishing.

Beaumont, B. (1999) 'Assessing risk in work with offenders.' In P. Parsloe (ed) *Risk Assessment in Social Care and Social Work*. London: Jessica Kingsley Publishers.

Beck, U. (1992) *Risk Society: Towards a New Modernity*. London: Sage.

Beck, U. (1998) 'Politics of risk society.' In J. Franklin (ed) *The Politics of Risk Society*. Cambridge: Polity.

Belcher, J., Doyle, S., Smart, C. and Stone K. (2003) 'Power to the people.' *Community Care 1502*, 11–17 Dec., 44–45.

Benbenishty, R., Osmo, R. and Gold, N. (2003) 'Rationales provided for risk assessments and for recommended interventions in child protection: A comparison between Canadian and Israeli professionals.' *British Journal of Social Work 33*, 2, 137–155.

Bennett, P. (2001) 'Understanding responses to risk: Some basic findings.' In P. Bennett and K. Calman (eds) *Risk Communication and Public Health*. Oxford: Oxford University Press.

Bennett, P. and Calman, K. (eds) (2001) *Risk Communication and Public Health*. Oxford: Oxford University Press.

Bentley, T. (1994) *Facilitation: Providing Opportunities for Learning*. London: McGraw Hill.

Beresford, P. (2003) 'Fully engaged.' *Community Care*, 13–19 Nov., 38–41.

Beresford, P. and Trevillion, S. (1995) *Developing Skills for Community Care: A Collaborative Approach.* Aldershot: Arena.

Berkowitz, S. (1991) *Key Findings from the State Survey Component of the Study of High Risk Child Abuse and Neglect Groups.* Washington, DC: National Center on Child Abuse and Neglect.

Bettesworth, C., Bettinis, J., Diamond, B., Morris, K. and Parkin, G. (2003) 'User involvement: Substance or spin?' *Journal of Mental Health 12*, 6, 613–626.

Bibby, P. (1994) *Personal Safety for Social Workers.* Aldershot: Arena.

Bolen, R.M. (2003) 'Child sexual abuse: Prevention or promotion?' *Social Work 48*, 2, 174–185.

Bond, H. (1998) 'Need to know.' *Community Care*, 12–18 Feb., 23.

Bowden, D. (1995) 'A priority in the health service.' *Managing Risk*, April, 1.

Brearley, C.P. (1979) 'Understanding risk.' *Social Work Today 10*, 31, 28.

Brearley, C.P. (1982) *Risk in Social Work.* London: Routledge and Kegan Paul.

Brown, H. (2002) *Vulnerability and Protection.* K202 Course Care Welfare and Community, Workbook Unit 18. Milton Keynes: Open University.

Burke, P. (1997) 'Risk and supervision: Social work responses to referred user problems.' *British Journal of Social Work 27*, 1, 115–129.

Burke, P. (1999) 'Social services staff: Risks they face and their dangerousness to others.' In P. Parsloe (ed) *Risk Assessment in Social Care and Social Work.* London: Jessica Kingsley Publishers.

Burns, S. and Bulman, C. (eds) (2000) *Reflective Practice in Nursing: The Growth of the Professional Practitioner.* Oxford: Blackwell.

Byrt, R. and Dooher, J. (2003) '"Service users" and "carers" and their desire for empowerment and participation.' In J. Dooher and R. Byrt (eds) *Empowerment and the Health Service User.* London: Quay Books.

Campbell, J.C. (ed) (1995) *Assessing Dangerousness: Violence by Sexual Offenders, Batterers and Child Abusers.* Thousand Oaks, CA: Sage.

Campbell, T.W. (2003) 'Sex offenders and actuarial risk assessments: Ethical considerations.' *Behavioral Sciences and the Law 21*, 2, 269–279.

Carson, D. (1988) 'Taking risks with patients: Your assessment strategy.' *Professional Nurse*, April, 247–250.

Carson, D. (ed) (1990) *Risk-taking in Mental Disorder: Analyses, Policies and Practical Strategies.* Chichester: SLE Publications.

Carson, D. (1995) 'Calculated risk.' *Community Care*, 26 Oct.–1 Nov., 26–27.

Carson, D. (1996) 'Risking legal repercussions.' In H. Kemshall and J. Pritchard (eds) *Good Practice in Risk Assessment and Risk Management*, vol. 1. London: Jessica Kingsley Publishers.

Carson, D. (1997) 'Good enough risk taking.' *International Review of Psychiatry 9*, 303–308.

Carson, D. (n.d.) 'Risk taking,' mimeo.

Central Council for Education and Training in Social Work (CCETSW) (1996) *Assuring Quality in the Diploma in Social Work – 1: Rules and regulations for the DipSW.* Revised. London: CCETSW.

Centre for Policy on Ageing (1984) *Home Life: A Code of Practice for Residential Care.* London: Centre for Policy on Ageing.

Centre for Policy on Ageing (1996) *A Better Home Life: A Code of Good Practice for Residential and Nursing Home Care.* London: Centre for Policy on Ageing.

Centre for Policy on Ageing (1999) *National Required Standards for Residential and Nursing Home Care.* London: Centre for Policy on Ageing.

Centre for Residential Child Care (1995) *Physical Restraint: Practice, Legal, Medical and Technical Considerations.* Glasgow: Centre for Residential Child Care.

Chitsabesan, P., Harrington, R., Harrington, V. and Tomenson, B. (2003) 'Predicting self-harm in children: How accurate can we expect to be?' *European Child and Adolescent Psychiatry 12*, 23–29.

Cieslik, M. and Pollock, G. (eds) (2002) *Young People in Risk Society: The Restructuring of Youth Identities and Transitions in Late Modernity.* Aldershot: Ashgate.

Clarke, C.L. and Heyman, B. (1998) 'Risk management for people with dementia.' In B. Heyman (ed) *Risk, Health and Health Care: A Qualitative Approach.* London: Arnold.

Clarke, C.L. (2000) 'Risk: Constructing care and care environments in dementia.' *Health, Risk and Society 2*, 1, 83–93.

Clements, L. (1996) *Community Care and the Law.* London: Legal Action Group.

Clements, L. and McDonald, A. (2002) *Using the Law*, K202 Course Care Welfare and Community, Workbook Unit 21. Milton Keynes: Open University.

Cohen, S. (1972) *Folk Devils and Moral Panics: The Creation of the Mods and Rockers.* London: Paladin.

Coles, D. (2001) 'The identification and management of risk: Opening up the process.' In P. Bennett and K. Calman (eds) *Risk Communication and Public Health.* Oxford: Oxford University Press.

Congress, E.P. (2000) 'What social workers should know about ethics: Understanding and resolving practice.' *Advances in Social Work 1,* 1, 1–25.

Connelly, N. (2002) *Assessing Need.* K202 Course Care Welfare and Community, Workbook Unit 10. Milton Keynes: Open University.

Cook, G. (1996) 'Risk taking in rehabilitative care: Professional and legal considerations.' *Health Care in Later Life 1,* 4–13.

Cook, G. and Procter, S. (1998) 'Risk: A nursing dilemma.' In B. Heyman (ed) *Risk, Health and Health Care: A Qualitative Approach.* London: Arnold.

Cooke, D. (2000) 'Current risk assessment instruments.' MacLean Committee *Report of the Committee on Serious Violent and Sexual Offenders (Annex 6).* Edinburgh: Scottish Executive.

Coote, A. (1998) 'Risk and public policy: Towards a high-trust democracy.' In J. Franklin (ed) *The Politics of Risk Society.* Cambridge: Polity.

Corby, B. (1996) 'Risk assessment in child protection work.' In H. Kemshall and J. Pritchard (eds) *Good Practice in Risk Assessment and Management.* London: Jessica Kingsley Publishers.

Corby, B. and Mills, C. (1986) 'Child abuse: Risks and resources.' *British Journal of Social Work 16,* 531–542.

Corfield, T. (1994) 'Risk assessment and health and safety management training.' *Modern Management 8,* 5, October, 10–12.

Corrado, R.R., Cohen, I.M. Glackman, W. and Odgers, C. (2003) 'Serious and violent young offenders' decisions to recidivate: An assessment of five sentencing models.' *Crime and Delinquency 49,* 2, 179–200.

Counsel and Care (1992) *What If They Hurt Themselves.* London: Counsel and Care.

Counsel and Care (1993) *The Right To Take Risks.* London: Counsel and Care.

Cowan, J. (2003) 'Risk management and the NSF for older people.' *Clinical Governance: An International Journal 8,* 1, 92–95.

CRAG/SCOTMEG Working Group on Mental Illness (1995) *Nursing Observation of Acutely Ill Psychiatric Patients in Hospital: A Good Practice Statement.* Edinburgh: Scottish Office.

Craissati, J. (1998) *Child Sexual Abusers: A Community Treatment Approach.* Hove: Psychology Press.

Crosland, J. (1992) *Risk Taking and Rights: Safety or Restraint?* Nursing Development Unit, Seacroft Hospital, Leeds.

Daniel, B. (2004) 'An overview of the Scottish multidisciplinary child protection review.' *Child and Family Social Work 9,* 3, 247–257.

Darjee, R. (2003) 'The reports of the Millan and MacLean committees: New proposals for mental health legislation and for high-risk offenders in Scotland.' *Journal of Forensic Psychiatry and Psychology 14,* 1, 7–28.

Darr, K. (1999) 'Risk management and quality improvement: Together at last – part 2.' *Hospital Topics 77,* 2, 29–35.

Davidson, G., McCallion, M. and Potter, M. (2003) *Connecting Mental Health and Human Rights.* Belfast: Northern Ireland Human Rights Commission.

Davidson-Arad, B., Englechin-Segal, D., Gabriel, R. and Wozner, Y. (2003) 'Why social workers do not implement decisions to remove children from home.' *Child Abuse and Neglect 27,* 6, 687–697.

Davis, A. (1996) 'Risk work and mental health.' In H. Kemshall and J. Pritchard (eds) *Good Practice in Risk Assessment and Risk Management,* vol. 1. London: Jessica Kingsley Publishers.

Davison, S. (1997) 'Risk assessment and management – a busy practitioner's perspective.' *International Review of Psychiatry 9,* 2/3, 201–206.

DePanfilis, D. and Zuravin, S.J. (2001) 'Assessing risk to determine the need for services.' *Children and Youth Services Review 23,* 1, 3–20.

Department of Constitutional Affairs (2004) *Notes on the Mental Capacity Bill.* London: Department of Constitutional Affairs.

Department for Education and Skills (2003) *Every Child Matters.* Green Paper. London: Stationery office.

Department for Education and Skills (2004) *Every Child Matters: The Next Steps.* London: Stationery Office.

Department of Health (1988) *Protecting Children: A Guide for Social Workers Undertaking a Comprehensive Assessment.* London: HMSO.

Department of Health (1996) *The Primary Care of Schizophrenia.* London: HMSO.

Department of Health (2000) *Framework for the Assessment of Children in Need and their Families.* London: Stationery Office.

Department of Health (2002) *Requirements For Social Work Training.* London: Stationery Office.

Department of Health (2003) *Memorandum to the Health Select Committee on Elder Abuse.* Minutes of Evidence EA21. London: House of Commons.

Department of Health (2004a) *Building A Better Future.* London: Stationery Office.

Department of Health (2004b) *Building a Better Future for Children. Key Messages from Inspection and Performance Assessment.* London: Stationery Office.

Department of Health (2004c) *Improving Mental Health Law. Towards a New Mental Health Act.* London: Stationery Office.

Department of Health and Home Office (2000) *No Secrets. Guidance on Developing and Implementing Multiagency Policies and Procedures to Protect Vulnerable Adults from Abuse.* London: Stationery Office.

Department of Health, Social Services and Public Safety (2003) *Specifications for the Degree in Social Work.* Belfast: DHSSPS.

Department of Trade and Industry (2004) *Fairness for All: A new Commission for Equality and Human Rights.* Cm6185. London: Stationery Office.

Dingwall, R. (2000) '"Risk Society": The cult of theory and the millenium?' In N. Manning and I. Shaw (eds) *New Risks, New Welfare.* Oxford: Blackwell.

Dryfoos, J.G. (1990) *Adolescents at Risk: Prevalence and Prevention.* New York: OUP.

Douglas, M. (1992) *Risk and Blame: Essays in Cultural Theory.* London: Routledge.

Douglas, M. and Calvez, M. (1990) 'The self as risk taker: A cultural theory of contagion in relation to AIDS.' *Sociological Review 38,* 445–464.

Duff, C. (2003) 'The importance of culture and context: Rethinking risk and risk management in young drug using populations.' *Health, Risk and Society 5,* 3, 285–299.

Dunbar, J. (1997) 'Making restraint-free care work.' *Provider,* May, 75–76.

East, J. (1995) 'Risk management in health care.' *British Journal of Health Care Management 1,* 3, 148–152.

Edwards, A., Elwyn, G. and Gwyn, R. (1999) 'General practice registrar responses to the use of different risk communication tools in simulated consultations: A focus group study.' *British Medical Journal 319,* 749–752.

Edwards, C. (2003) 'The involvement of service users in the assessment of diploma in social work students on practice placements.' *Social Work Education 22,* 4, 341–349.

English, D.J. and Pecora, P.J. (1994) 'Risk assessment as a practice method in child protective services.' *Child Welfare 73,* 5, 451–473.

Evans, L.K. and Strumpf, N.E. (1989) 'Tying down the elderly: A review of the literature on physical restraints.' *Journal of American Geriatric Society 37,* 65–74.

Fabb, J. and Guthrie, T.G. (1997) *Social Work and the Law in Scotland.* 2nd ed. Edinburgh: Butterworths.

Feaviour, P., Peacock, D., Sanderson, H., Bontoft, C. and Wightman, S. (1995) 'Score values.' *Community Care,* 2–8 November, 28–29.

Fisher, M., Newton, C. and Sainsbury, E. (1984) *Mental Health Social Work Observed.* London: Allen and Unwin.

Fisher, W.A. (1994) 'Restraint and Seclusion: A review of the literature.' *American Journal of Psychiatry 151,* 11, 1584–1591.

Fowler, A. (1993) 'How to evaluate training.' *Personnel Management Plus 4,* 9 September, 25–26.

Franklin, J. (ed) (1998) *The Politics of Risk Society.* Cambridge: Polity.

French, S. and Maule, J. (2001) 'Improving risk communication: Scenario-based workshops.' In P. Bennett and K. Calman (eds) *Risk Communication and Public Health.* Oxford: Oxford University Press.

Gale, T.M., Hawley J. and Sivakumaran, T. (2003) 'Do mental health professionals really understand probability? Implications for risk assessment and evidence-based practice.' *Journal of Mental Health 12,* 4, 417–430.

Gale, T.M., Woodward, A., Hawley, C.J., Hayes, J., Sivakumaran, T. and Hansen, T. (2002) 'Risk assessment for people with mental health problems: A pilot study of reliability in working practice.' *International Journal of Psychiatry in Clinical Practice 6,* 73–81.

Gambrill, E. and Shlonsky, A. (2000) 'Risk assessment in context.' *Children and Youth Services Review 22,* 11/12, 813–837.

Gambrill, E. and Shlonsky, A. (2001) 'The need for comprehensive risk management systems in child welfare.' *Children and Youth Services Review 23,* 1, 79–107.

Garrett, P.M. (2003) 'Swimming with dolphins: The Assessment Framework, New Labour and new tools for social work with children and families.' *British Journal of Social Work 33,* 4, 441–463.

George, M. (1997a) 'Independence Day.' *Community Care,* 1–7 May, 38–39.

George, M. (1997b) 'Clean-up operation.' *Community Care,* 5–11 June, 36–37.

George, M. (1998a) 'Sliding into dementia.' *Community Care*, 7–13 May, 32–33.

George, M. (1998b) 'Quality living.' *Community Care*, 6–12 June, 34–35.

Giddens, A. (1998) 'Risk society: The context of British politics.' In J. Franklin (ed) *The Politics of Risk Society.* Cambridge: Polity.

Giliker, P. and Beckwith, S. (2000) *Tort.* London: Sweet and Maxwell.

Gilmour, H., Gibson, F. and Campbell, J. (2003) 'Living alone with dementia: A case study approach to understanding risk.' *Dementia 2*, 3, 403–420.

Gorman, H. (2003) 'Which skills do care managers need? A research project on skills, competency and continuing professional development.' *Social Work Education 22*, 3, 245–260.

Gough, D. (1993) 'The current literature about organised abuse of children.' *Child Abuse Review 2*, 4, 281–287.

Gould, N. and Taylor, I. (eds) (1996) *Reflective Learning for Social Work.* Aldershot: Arena.

Green, L. and Masson, H. (2002) 'Adolescents who sexually abuse and residential accommodation: Issues of risk and vulnerability.' *British Journal of Social Work 32*, 2, 149–168.

Greenland, C. (1987) *Preventing CAN Deaths: An International Study of Deaths Due to Child Abuse and Neglect.* London: Tavistock.

Griffiths, R. and Waterston, J. (1996) 'Facts, fantasies and confusion: Risk and substance use.' In H. Kemshall and J. Pritchard (eds) *Good Practice in Risk Assessment and Risk Management*, vol. 1. London: Jessica Kingsley Publishers.

Grubin, D. (1997) 'Inferring predictors of risk: Sex offenders.' *International Review of Psychiatry 9*, 225–231.

Gunn, J. (1997) 'Maintaining a balanced perspective on risk.' *International Review of Psychiatry 9*, 163–165.

Hanson, R.K. and Bussière, M.T. (1996) *Predictions of Sex Offender Recidivism: A Meta-analysis.* User Report 96-04. Ontario, Ottawa: Department of the Solicitor General of Canada.

Halstead, S. (1997) 'Risk assessment and management in psychiatric practice: Inferring predictors of risk. A view from learning disability.' *International Review of Psychiatry 9*, 2/3, 217–224.

Harris, A. (2000) 'Risk management in practice: How are we managing?' *Clinical Performance and Quality Health Care 8*, 3, 142–149.

Harris, J. (1996) 'Physical restraint procedures for managing challenging behaviours presented by mentally retarded children and adults.' *Research in Developmental Disabilities 17*, 99–134.

Harris, J., Allen, D., Cornick, M., Jefferson, A. and Mills, R. (1996) *A Policy Framework to Guide the Use of Physical Interventions (Restrain) with Adults and Children with Learning Disability and/or Autism.* Kidderminster: British Institute for Learning Disabilities.

Harris, M. (1997) 'Training trainers in risk assessment.' *British Journal of Psychiatry 170*, suppl. 32, 35–36.

Harrison, D. (2002) 'Health promotion and politics.' In R. Bunton and G. Macdonald (eds) *Health Promotion: Disciplines, Diversity and Developments.* London: Routledge.

Harrison, L. (1997) 'Risk assessment in a climate of litigation.' *British Journal of Psychiatry 170*, suppl. 32, 37–39.

Harrer, R. and Thom, B. (1997) 'The right to take risks: Alcohol and older people.' *Social Policy and Administration 31*, 3, 233–246.

Health and Safety Executive (1997) *Risk Assessment at Work: Practical Examples in the NHS.* London: HSE

Health and Safety Executive (1998) *Five Steps to Risk Assessment.* London: HSE

Health Education Authority (1998) *Promoting the Health of Children and Young People: Setting a Research Agenda.* London: HEA.

Heyman, B. (ed) (1998) *Risk, Health and Health Care: A Qualitative Approach.* London: Arnold.

Hier, S.P. (2003) 'Risk and panic in late modernity: Implications of the converging sites of social anxiety.' *British Journal of Sociology 51*, 1, 3–20.

Hill, M. and Aldgate, J. (eds) (1996) *Child Welfare Services: Developments in Law, Policy, Practice and Research.* London: Jessica Kingsley Publishers.

Holloway, F. (1997) 'The assessment and management of risk in psychiatry: Can we do better?' *Psychiatric Bulletin 21*, 5, 283–285.

Hopkins, G. (2003) 'Freezing cold and all alone.' *Community Care*, 30 Oct.–5 Nov., 42–43.

Hopkins, G. (2004a) 'Honesty wins the day.' *Community Care*, 5–11 Feb., 46–47.

Hopkins, G. (2004b) 'In defiance of the family.' *Community Care*, 1–7 Apr., 48–49.

Hopkins, G. (2004c) 'In denial of abuse.' *Community Care*, 6–12 May, 46–47.

Hopkins, G. (2004d) 'The healthy whole.' *Community Care*, 15–21 Apr., 38–39.

Hopson, B. and Scally, M. (1980) *Lifeskills Teaching Programmes, No 1.* Leeds: Lifeskills Associates.

Hopson, B. and Scally, M. (1982) *Lifeskills Teaching Programmes, No 2.* Leeds: Lifeskills Associates.

Hopson, B. and Scally, M. (1986) *Lifeskills Teaching Programmes, No 3.* Leeds: Lifeskills Associates.

Horsefield, A. (2003) 'Risk assessment: Who needs it?' *Probation Journal 50,* 4, 374–379.

House of Commons Health Committee (2004) *Elder Abuse.* Second report of session 2003–2004. Volume 1 HCIII-I and Volume 2 HCIII-II. London: Stationery Office.

Houston, S. and Griffiths, H. (2000) 'Reflections on risk in child protection: Is it time for a shift in paradigms?' *Child and Family Social Work 5,* 1–10.

Howard League (1985) *Unlawful Sex: Offences, Victims and Offenders in the Criminal Justice System of England and Wales.* London: Waterlow.

Howlett, M. (1997) 'Community care homicide inquiries and risk assessment.' In H. Kemshall and J. Pritchard (eds) *Good Practice in Risk Assessment and Management.* London: Jessica Kingsley Publishers.

Hui-Chi, H., Meei-Ling, G., Wen-Chuan, L. and Kernohan, G. (2003) 'Assessing risk of falling in older adults.' *Public Health Nursing 20,* 5, 399–411.

Inskip, H.M., Harris, E.C. and Barraclough, B. (1998) 'Lifetime risk of suicide for affective disorder, alcoholism and schizophrenia.' *British Journal of Psychiatry 172,* 35–37.

Jackson, A. and Hyslop, J. (2003) 'User empowerment and user involvement in mental health.' In J. Dooher and R. Byrt (eds) *Empowerment and the Health Service User.* London: Quay Books.

Jackson, W. (1992) *Risk Taking, Safety and Older People: Selected Bibliography on Ageing.* London: Centre for Policy on Ageing.

Joffe, H. (1999) *Risk and the Other.* Cambridge: Cambridge University Press.

Jung, S. and Rawana, E.P. (1999) 'Risk and need assessment of juvenile offenders.' *Criminal Justice and Behavior 26,* 1, 69–89.

Kaliski, S.Z. (1997) 'Risk management during the transition from hospital to community care.' *International Review of Psychiatry 9,* 249–256.

Kelly, G. (1996) 'Competence in risk analysis.' In K. O'Hagan (ed) *Competence in Social Work Practice.* London: Jessica Kingsley Publishers.

Kelly, T., Simmons, W. and Gregory, E. (2002) 'Risk assessment and management: A community forensic mental health practice model.' *International Journal of Mental Health Nursing 11,* 206–213.

Kemshall, H. (1996) 'Offender risk and probation practice.' In H. Kemshall and J. Pritchard (eds) *Good Practice in Risk Assessment and Risk Management,* vol. 1. London: Jessica Kingsley Publishers.

Kemshall, H. (2000) 'Conflicting knowledges on risk: The case of risk knowledge in the probation service.' *Health, Risk and Society 2,* 2, 143–158.

Kemshall, H. (2002a) *Risk Assessment and Management of Serious Violent and Sexual Offenders: A Review of Current Issues.* Edinburgh: Scottish Executive.

Kemshall, H. (2002b) *Risk, Social Policy and Welfare.* Buckingham: Open University Press.

Kemshall, H., Parton, N., Walsh, M. and Waterson, J. (1997) 'Concepts of risk in relation to organisational structure and functioning within the personal social services and probation.' *Social Policy and Administration 31,* 3, 213–232.

Kemshall, H. and Pritchard, J. (eds) (1996) *Good Practice in Risk Assessment and Risk Management,* vol. 1. London: Jessica Kingsley Publishers.

Kemshall, H. and Pritchard, J. (eds) (1997) *Good Practice in Risk Assessment and Risk Management,* vol. 2. London: Jessica Kingsley Publishers.

Kennedy, M. and Gill, M. (1997) 'Patient litigation following a homicide – implications for the assessment and management of risk.' *International Review of Psychiatry 9,* 179–186.

Kinnair, D. (2003) 'Child protection: Lessons from the recent past.' *Community Practitioner 76,* 4, 121–122.

Landau, R. (2000) 'Ethical dilemmas in general hospitals: Social workers' contribution to ethical decision-making.' *Social Work in Health Care 32,* 2, 75–92.

Langan, J. (1991) 'A common practice.' *Community Care,* 24 October, 19–21.

Langan, J. (1999) 'Assessing risk in mental health.' In P. Parsloe (ed) *Risk Assessment in Social Care and Social Work.* London: Jessica Kingsley Publishers.

Lash, S., Szerszynski, B. and Wynne, B. (1996) *Risk, Environment and Modernity: Towards a New Ecology.* London: Sage.

Law Society of Scotland, Royal College of Psychiatrists, Scottish Division and Scottish Association for Mental Health (1996) *The Mental Health (Scotland) Act: Consensus for change?* Edinburgh: Law Society of Scotland. Royal College of Psychiatrists, Scottish Division and Scottish Association for Mental Health.

Lawson, J. (1996) 'A framework of risk assessment and management for older people.' In H. Kemshall and J. Pritchard (eds) *Good Practice in Risk Assessment and Management.* London: Jessica Kingsley Publishers.

Leathard, A. (2003) *Interprofessional Collaboration: From Policy to Practice in Health and Social Care.* Hove: Brunner-Routledge.

Lefevre, F.V., Waters, T.M. and Budetti, P.P. (2000) 'A survey of physician training programs in risk management and communication skills for malpractice prevention.' *Journal of Law, Medicine and Ethics 28,* 3, 258–246.

Little, M., Axford, N. and Morpeth, L. (2004) Research review: Risk and protection in the context of services for children in need.' *Child and Family Social Work 9,* 1, 105–117.

Littlechild, B. (1996) 'Violence and agression to social work and social care staff.' In H. Kemshall and J. Pritchard (eds) *Good Practice in Risk Assessment and Risk Management,* vol. 1. London: Jessica Kingsley Publishers.

Littlechild, R. and Blakeney, J. (1996) 'Risk and older people.' In H. Kemshall and J. Pritchard (eds) *Good Practice in Risk Assessment and Risk Management,* vol. 1. London: Jessica Kingsley Publishers.

Lordan, N. (2000) 'Finding a voice: Empowerment of people with disabilities in Ireland.' *Journal of Progressive Human Services 11,* 1, 49–69.

Lord Chancellor's Department (1997) *Who Decides? Making Decisions on Behalf of Mentally Incapacitated Adults.* London: Lord Chancellor's Department.

Loucks, N. (2002) *Recidivism amongst Serious Violent and Sexual Offenders.* Edinburgh: Scottish Executive.

Lyon, J. (1997) 'Teenage suicide and self-harm: Assessing and managing risk.' In H. Kemshall and J. Pritchard (eds) *Good Practice in Risk Assessment and Risk Management,* vol. 2. London: Jessica Kingsley Publishers.

Macdonald, K.I. and Macdonald, G.M. (1999) 'Perceptions of risk.' In P. Parsloe (ed) *Risk Assessment in Social Care and Social Work.* London: Jessica Kingsley Publishers.

MacLean Committee (2000) *Report of the Committee on Serious Violent and Sexual Offenders.* Edinburgh: Scottish Executive.

Maggs, J.L., Frome, P.M., Eccles, J.S. and Barber, B.L. (1997) 'Psychosocial resources, adolescent risk behaviour and young adult adjustment: Is risk taking more dangerous for some than others?' *Journal of Adolescence 20,* 103–119.

Manchester Open Learning Project (1993) *Negotiation.* Manchester: Manchester Open Learning Project.

Manning, N. (1987) 'What is a social problem?' In M. Loney, D. Boswell and J. Clarke (eds) *Social Problems and Social Welfare.* London, Sage.

Manthorpe, J. and Stanley, N. (2002) *Risk and Dangerousness.* K202 Course Care Welfare and Community, Workbook Unit 19. Milton Keynes: Open University.

Manthorpe, J., Walsh, M., Alaszewski, A. and Harrison, L. (1995), 'Taking a chance.' *Community Care,* 19–25 October, 20–21.

Manthorpe, J., Walsh, M., Alaszewski, A. and Harrison, L. (1997) 'Issues of risk practice and welfare in learning disability services.' *Disability and Society 12,* 69–82.

McDonald, A. (2004) *Community Care Law: Social Work File.* 2nd ed. Norwich: University of East Anglia.

McEwan, S. and Sullivan, J. (1996) 'Sex offender risk assessment.' In H. Kemshall and J. Pritchard (eds) *Good Practice in Risk Assessment and Risk Management* vol. 1. London: Jessica Kingsley Publishers.

McHale, J. and Tingle, J. (2001) *Law and Nursing.* Oxford: Butterworth Heinemann.

McIvor, G., Kemshall, H. and Levy, G. (2002) *Serious Violent and Sexual Offenders: The Use of Risk Assessment Tools in Scotland.* Edinburgh: Scottish Executive.

McKay, C. and Patrick, H. (1995) *The Care Maze.* Glasgow: Enable and SAMH.

McLennan, A.T., Hagan, T.A., Levine, M., Gould, F., Meyers, K., Bencivengo, M. and Durell, J. (1998) 'Supplemental social services improve outcomes in public addiction treatment.' *Addiction 93,* 10, 1489–1499.

McWilliam, C. and Coleman, S. (2003) 'Building empowering partnerships for interprofessional care.' *Journal of Interprofessional Care 17,* 4, 363–376.

Mental Health Reference Group (2000) *Risk Management.* Edinburgh: Scottish Executive.

Mental Welfare Commission for Scotland (1998) *Restraint of Residents with Mental Impairment in Care Homes and Hospitals.* Edinburgh: Mental Welfare Commission for Scotland.

Mohr, W.K. and Anderson, J.A. (2001) 'Faulty assumptions associated with the use of restraints with children.' *Journal of Child and Adolescent Psychiatric Nursing 14,* 141–151.

Mohr, W.K., Petti, T.A. and Mohr, B.D. (2003) 'Adverse effects associated with physical restraint.' *Canadian Journal of Psychiatry 48,* 330–337.

Monahan, J. (1988) 'Risk assessment of violence among the mentally disordered: Generating useful knowledge.' *International Journal of Law and Psychiatry 11,* 249–57.

Moore, S. and Parsons, J. (2000) 'A research agenda for adolescent risk-taking: Where do we go from here?' *Journal of Adolescence 23*, 4, 371–376.

Morgan, S. (2000) 'Risk-making or risk-taking?' *OpenMind 101*, Jan./Feb., 16–17.

Munson, C.E. (1996) 'Risk management in mental health practice.' *Clinical Supervisor 14*, 1, 1–17.

Murphy, S. (1996) 'Managing the risk.' *Health and Safety at Work 18*, 7, July, 18–20.

Murphy, W.D., Haynes, M.R. and Worley, P.J. (1991) 'Assessment of adult sexual interest.' In C.R. Hollin and K. Howells (eds) *Clinical Approaches to Sex Offenders and their Victims.* Chichester: Wiley.

Nash, M. (1998) 'Managing risk – achieving protection? The police and probation agendas.' *International Journal of Public Sector Management 11*, 4/5, 252–261.

National Commission of Inquiry into the Prevention of Child Abuse (2004) *Childhood Matters: Report of Commission,* vol. 1. London: Stationery Office.

Norman, A. (1980) *Rights and Risk.* London: Centre for Policy on Ageing.

Norman, A. (1987) *Severe Dementia: The Provision of Longstay Care.* London: Centre for Policy on Ageing.

Norman, A. (1988) 'Risk.' In B. Gearing, M. Johnson and T. Heller (eds) *Mental Health Problems in Old Age: A Reader.* Chichester: Wiley.

North West London Mental Health NHS Trust (1994) *Report of the Independent Panel of Inquiry Examining the Case of Michael Buchanan.* London: North West London Mental Health NHS Trust.

Northern Ireland Social Care Council (2002) *Code of Practice for Social Care Workers.* Belfast: NISCC.

Nursing Development Unit Seacroft Hospital (n.d.), Charters and leaflets. Leeds: Seacroft Hospital.

Nursing and Midwifery Council (2002) *Code of Professional Conduct: Protecting the Public Through Professional Standards.* London: Nursing and Midwifery Council.

Oakley, P. and Taylor, R. (1994) 'An approach to developing risk-conscious staff.' *Health Service Journal 107*, 7, July, 5–7.

O'Callaghan, D. and Print, B. (1994) 'Adolescent Sexual Abusers: Research, assessment and treatment.' In T. Morrison, M. Erooga and R. Beckett (eds) *Sexual Offenders Against Children: Practice, Management and Policy.* London: Routledge.

O'Sullivan, T. (1999) *Decision Making in Social Work.* Basingstoke: Macmillan

Oliver, J. and Scott, T. (1996) 'Trouble with training.' *British Journal of Health Care Management 2*, 7, July, 388–391.

O'Rourke, M. and Bird, L. (2001) *Risk Management in Mental Health.* London: Mental Health Foundation.

Ovretveit, J., Mathais, P. and Thompson, T. (1997) *Interprofessional Working for Health and Social Care.* Baskingstoke: Macmillan.

Parsloe, P. (1999a) 'Introduction.' In P. Parsloe (ed) *Risk Assessment in Social Care and Social Work.* London: Jessica Kingsley Publishers.

Parsloe, P. (1999b) (ed) *Risk Assessment in Social Care and Social Work.* London: Jessica Kingsley Publishers.

Parton, N. (1996) 'Social work, risk and the "blaming system".' In N. Parton (ed) *Social Theory, Social Change and Social Work.* London: Routledge.

Parton, N. (1998) 'Risk, advanced liberalism and child welfare: The need to rediscover uncertainty and ambiguity.' *British Journal of Social Work 28*, 5–27.

Parton, N., Thorpe, D. and Wattam, C. (1997) *Child Protection: Risk and the Moral Order.* Basingstoke: Macmillan.

Patrick, H. (1996) In Law Society of Scotland, Royal College of Psychiatrists, Scottish Division and Scottish Association for Mental Health (1996) *The Mental Health (Scotland) Act: Consensus for change?* Edinburgh: Law Society of Scotland. Royal College of Psychiatrists, Scottish Division and Scottish Association for Mental Health.

Pearce, I.D. (1995) *The Assessment and Evaluation of Training: A Practical Guide.* Hitchin: Technical Communications (Publishing).

Pearce, I.D. (1997) 'Has your training been worthwhile?' *Training Officer 33*, 1, 5–7.

Peterson, A.C. and Leffert, N. (1995) 'Developmental issues in influencing guidelines for adolescent health research: A review.' *Journal of Adolescent Health 17*, 298–305.

Petrila, J. (2004) 'Emerging issues in forensic mental health.' *Psychiatric Quarterly 75*, 1, 3–21.

Petrunik, M.G. (2002) 'Managing unacceptable risk: Sex offenders, community response and social policy in the United States and Canada.' *International Journal of Offender Therapy and Comparative Criminology 46*, 4, 483–511.

Pilgrim, D. and Rogers, A. (1996) 'Two conceptions of risk in mental health debates.' In T. Heller, J. Reynolds, R. Gomm, R. Muston and S. Pattison (eds) *Mental Health Matters: A Reader.* Basingstoke: Macmillan.

Plant, M. and Plant, M. (1992) *Risk Takers: Alcohol, Drugs, Sex and Youth.* London: Tavistock/Routledge.

Pout, T. (1966) *Developing Effective Training Skills: A Practical Guideline to Developing and Delivering Group Training.* London: McGraw-Hill.

Potts, J. (1995) 'Risk assessment and management: A Home Office perspective.' In J. Crichton (ed) *Psychiatric Patient Violence: Risk and Response.* London: Duckworth.

Powell, J.L. and Edwards, M. (2003) 'Risk and youth: A critical sociological perspective.' *International Journal of Sociology and Social Policy 23*, 12, 81–94.

Preston-Shoot, M. (2001) 'Evaluating self-determination: An adult protection case study. *Journal of Adult Protection 3*, 1, 4–14.

Priestley, P., Flegg, D., Hemsley, V., Welham, D. and McGuire, J. (1978) *Social Skills and Personal Problem Solving: A Handbook of Methods.* London: Tavistock.

Prins, H. (1996) 'Risk assessment and management in criminal justice and psychiatry.' *Journal of Forensic Psychiatry 7*, 1, 42–62.

Pritchard, J. (1995) *Abuse of Older People.* London: Jessica Kinglsey Publishers.

Pritchard, J. (1997) 'Vulnerable people taking risks: Older people and residential care.' In H. Kemshall and J. Pritchard (eds) *Good Practice in Risk Assessment and Risk Management*, vol. 2. London: Jessica Kingsley Publishers.

Pritchard, S. and Brearley, P. (1982) 'Risk in social work.' In C.P. Brearley *Risk and Ageing.* London: Routledge and Kegan Paul.

Rae, L. (1986) *How To Measure Training Effectiveness.* Aldershot: Gower.

Rae, L. (1995) 'Practical approaches to evaluation.' *Training Officer 31*, 9, 273–276.

Raynor, P., Kyash, J., Roberts, C. and Merrington, S. (2002) *Two Risk and Need Assessment Instruments Used in Probation Services.* Research Findings 143. London: Home Office.

Reamer, F.G. (1983) 'Ethical dilemmas in social work practice.' *Social Work 28*, 1, 31–35.

Reed, J. (1997) 'Risk assessment and clinical risk management: The lessons from recent inquiries.' *British Journal of Psychiatry 170*, suppl. 32, 4–7.

Regester, M. and Larkin, J. (2002) *Risk Issues and Crisis Management: A Casebook of Best Practice.* London: Kogan Page.

Reith, K.A. and Bennett, C.C. (1998) 'Restraint free care.' *Nursing Management*, May.

Ritchie, J.H., Dick, D. and Lingham, R. (1994) *The Report of the Inquiry into the Care and Treatment of Christopher Clunis.* London: HMSO.

Roberts, C.F., Doren, D.M. and Thorton D. (2002) 'Dimensions associated with assessments of sex offender recidivism risk.' *Criminal Justice and Behavior 29*, 5, 569–589.

Robinson, D. and Collins, M. (1999) 'Risk assessment: A challenge to nurses and nurse managers.' *Mental Health Practice 2*, 6, 8–13.

Rogers, W.V.H. (2002) *Winfield and Jolowicz on Tort.* London: Sweet and Maxwell.

Rossau, C.D. and Mortensen, P.B. (1997) 'Risk factors for suicide in patients with schizophrenia: Nested case-control study.' *British Journal of Psychiatry 171*, 355–359.

Royal Society (1992) *Risk Analysis, Perception and Management.* London: Royal Society.

Rubenstein, L.V., Calkins, D., Greenfield, S., Jette, A., Meenau, R., Nevins, M., Rubenstein, L.Z., Wasson, J. and Williams, M. (1989) 'Health status assessment for elderly patients: Report of the society of general internal medicine task force on health assessment.' *Journal of the American Geriatrics Society 37*, 562–569.

Rutter, M. (1993) 'Resilience: Some conceptual considerations.' *Journal of Adolescent Health 14*, 626–631.

Ryan, T. (1996) 'Risk management and people with mental health problems.' In H. Kemshall and J. Pritchard (eds) *Good Practice in Risk Assessment and Risk Management.* London: Jessica Kingsley Publishers.

Ryan, T. (1997) 'Risk, residential service and people with mental health needs.' In H. Kemshall and J. Pritchard (eds) *Good Practice in Risk Assessment and Risk Management*, vol. 2. London: Jessica Kingsley Publishers.

Ryan, T. (2000) 'Exploring the risk management strategies of mental health services users.' *Health, Risk and Society 2*, 3, 267–282.

Sameroff, A. (2001) 'Ecological perspectives on developmental risk.' In J.D. Osofsky and H.E. Fitzgerald (eds) *Infant Mental Health in Groups at High Risk*, vol. 4. World Association for Infant Mental Health Handbook of Infant Mental Health. New York: Wiley.

Sargent, K. (1999) 'Assessing risks for children.' In P. Parsloe (ed) *Risk Assessment in Social Care and Social Work.* London: Jessica Kingsley Publishers.

Saunders, B. and Goddard, C.R. (1998) *A Critique of Structured Risk Assessment Procedures: Instruments of Abuse?* Melbourne: Child Abuse and Family Violence Research Unit, Monash University.

Scheflin, A.W. (1998) 'Risk management in treating child sexual abuse victims and adult survivors.' *Journal of Child Sexual Abuse 7*, 1, 111–121.

Schon, D. (1983) *The Reflective Practitioner.* San Fransisco: Jossey Bass.

Scott, D. (1998) 'A qualitative study of social work assessment in cases of alleged child abuse.' *British Journal of Social Work 28,* 73–88.

Scottish Executive (2001) *New Directions: Report on the Review of the Mental Health (Scotland) Act 1984.* Edinburgh: Scottish Executive.

Scottish Executive (2002) *It's Everyone's Job To Make Sure I'm Alright. Report of the Child Protection Audit and Review.* Edinburgh: Scottish Executive.

Scottish Executive (2003) *The Framework for Social Work Education in Scotland.* Edinburgh: Scottish Executive.

Scottish Executive (2004a) *Getting It Right for Every Child: Review of the Children's Hearings System.* Edinburgh: Scottish Executive.

Scottish Executive (2004b) *National Care Standards. Care Homes for Children and Young People.* Edinburgh: Socttish Executive.

Scottish Executive (2004c) *National Care Standards. Care Homes for Older People.* Edinburgh: Socttish Executive.

Scottish Executive (2004d) *National Care Standards. Care Homes for People with Learning Difficulties.* Edinburgh: Socttish Executive.

Scottish Executive (2004e) *Protecting Children and Young People: Framework for Standards.* Edinburgh: Scottish Executive.

Scottish Executive (2004f) *Sharing Information About Children At Risk: A Guide to Good Practice.* Edinburgh: Scottish Executive.

Scottish Law Commission (1996) *Incapable Adults.* Report no. 151. Edinburgh.

Scottish Office (1997a) *A Commitment to Protect – Supervising Sex Offenders: Proposals for More Effective Practice.* Edinburgh: The Stationery Office.

Scottish Office (1997b) *Scotland's Children: The Children (Scotland) Act 1995 Regulations and Guidance: Volume 1: Support and Protection for Children and their Families.* Edinburgh: The Stationery Office.

Scottish Office (1998) *Risk Assessment: A Supplement to the National Objectives and Standards for Social Work Services in the Criminal Justice System.* Circular. Edinburgh: Scottish Office.

Scottish Social Services Council (2003) *Codes of Practice for Social Service Workers and Employers.* Dundee: Scottish Social Services Council.

Scottish Social Work Services Inspectorate (2004) *Report of the Inspection of Scottish Borders Council Social Work Services for People affected by Learning Disability.* Edinburgh: Scottish Executive.

Scourfield, J. and Welsh, I. (2003) 'Risk, reflexivity and social control in child protection: New times or same old story?' *Critical Social Policy 23,* 3, 398–420.

Secker-Walker, J. (1997) 'Risk management.' *British Journal of Hospital Medicine 58,* 8, 366–367.

Selekman, J. and Snyder, B. (1997) 'Institutional policies on the use of physical restraints on children.' *Pediatric Nursing 23,* 5, 531–537.

Sheppard, M. (1990) *Mental Health – The Role of the Approved Social Worker.* Sheffield: Joint Unit for Social Services Research.

Shlonsky, A. and Gambrill, E. (2001) 'The assessment and management of risk in child welfare services.' *Children and Youth Services Review 23,* 1–2.

Simon, R.I. (1998) 'Psychiatrists' duties in discharging sicker and potentially violent inpatients in the managed care era.' *Psychiatric Services 49,* 1, 62–67.

Sinclair, R. and Bullock, R. (2002) *Learning From Past Experience: A Review of Serious Case Reviews.* London: Department of Health.

Skeem, J.L., Mulvey, E.P., Applebaum, P., Banks, S., Grisso, T., Silver, E. and Robbins, P.C. (2004) 'Identifying subtypes of civil psychiatric patients at high risk for violence.' *Criminal Justice and Behavior, 31,* 4, 392–437.

Smith, G. (1997) 'Risk assessment and management at the interface between the probation service and psychiatric practice.' *International Review of Psychiatry 9,* 2/3, 283–288.

Smith, M. (2001) 'Risk assessment in mental health work.' *Practice 13,* 2, 21–30.

Soltys, S.M. (1995) 'Risk management strategies in the provision of mental health services.' *Psychiatric Services 5,* 46, 473–476.

Stalker, K. (2003) 'Managing risk and uncertainty in social work: A literature review.' *Journal of Social Work 3,* 2, 211–233.

Stanley, N. and Manthorpe, J. (1997) 'Risk assessment: Developing training for professionals in mental health work.' *Social Work and Social Sciences Review 7,* 1, 26–38.

Steadman, H.J., Monahan, J., Robbins, P.C., Applebaum, P., Grisso, T., Klassen, D., Mulvey, E.P. and Roth, L. (1993) 'From dangerousness to risk assessment: Implications for appropriate research strategies.' In S. Hodgins (ed) *Mental Disorder and Crime*. Newbury Park: Sage.

Stevenson, O. (1996) *Elder Protection in the Community: What Can We Learn from Child Protection?* London: Age Concern Institute of Gerontology.

Stevenson, O. (1999a) *Elder Protection in Residential Care: What Can We Learn from Child Protection?* London: Department of Health.

Stevenson, O. (1999b) 'Old people at risk.' In P. Parsloe (ed) *Risk Assessment in Social Care and Social Work*. London: Jessica Kingsley Publishers.

Stockwell, T. and Toubourou, J.W. (2004) 'Risk and protection factors for different intensities of adolescent substance use: When does the Prevention Paradox apply?' *Drug and Alcohol Review 23*, 1, 66–77.

Strand, S., Belfrage, H., Frausson, G. and Levander, S. (1999) 'Clinical and risk management factors in risk prediction of mentally disordered offenders – more important than historical data? A retrospective study of 40 mentally disordered offenders assessed with the HCR-20 violence risk assessment scheme.' *Legal and Criminological Psychology 4*, 1, 67–76.

Suckling, R., Ferris, M. and Price, C. (2003) 'Risk identification, assessment and management in one public health practice: A practical approach in one public health department.' *Journal of Public Health Medicine 25*, 2, 138–143.

Talbot, C. (1992) 'Evaluation and validation: A mixed approach.' *Journal of European Industrial Training 16*, 5, 26–32.

Tanner, D. (1998) 'The jeopardy of risk.' *Practice 10*, 1, 15–28.

Taylor, C. and Meux, C. (1997) 'Individual cases: The risk, the challenge.' *International Review of Psychiatry 9*, 289–302.

Taylor-Gooby, P. (2001) 'Risk, contingency and the Third Way: Evidence from the BHPS and qualitative studies.' *Social Policy and Administration 35*, 2, 195–211.

Taylor-Gooby, P., Dean, H., Munro, M. and Parker, G. (1999) 'Risk and the welfare state.' *British Journal of Sociology 50*, 2, 177–194.

Thompson, A. (1998) 'Reasons to be fearful.' *Community Care*, Nov. 26, 30–31.

Thornton, P (1992) 'A framework for the assessment of sex offenders.' Paper presented at 3rd European conference on Psychology and the Law, Oxford.

Tindall, B. (1997) 'People with learning difficulties: Citzenship, personal development and the management of risk.' In H. Kemshall and J. Pritchard (eds) *Good Practice in Risk Assessment and Risk Management*, vol. 2. London: Jessica Kingsley Publishers.

Tingle, J. (2002a) 'An introduction to clinical negligence: Nurses and the law.' *British Journal of Nursing 11*, 15, 1033–1035.

Tingle, J. (2002b) 'Understanding the legal duty of care in the course of negligence.' *British Journal of Nursing 11*, 16, 1065–1067.

Tingle, J. (2002c) 'Establishing breach of the duty of care in the tort of negligence.' *British Journal of Nursing 11*, 17, 1128–1130.

Tingle, J. (2002d) 'Establishing breach of the duty of care in the tort of negligence: 2.' *British Journal of Nursing 11*, 18, 1212–1214.

Titterton, M. (1991) 'Caring for mentally disabled people in Scotland.' *Social Policy and Administration 25*, 2, 137–148.

Titterton, M. (1992) 'Managing threats to welfare: The search for a new paradigm of welfare.' *Journal of Social Policy 21*, 1, 1–23.

Titterton, M. (1994) 'Managing change and innovation in community care.' In M. Titterton (ed) *Caring for People in the Community: The New Welfare*. London: Jessica Kingsley Publishers.

Titterton, M. (1997) *Assessing Risks And Managing Aggressive Behaviour and Violence*. Manual for Shetland Islands Council Social Work Department. Lerwick: Shetland Islands Council.

Titterton, M. (1999) 'Training professionals in risk assessment and risk management: What does the research tell us?' In P. Parsloe (ed) *Risk Assessment in Social Care and Social Work*. London: Jessica Kingsley Publishers.

Titterton, M. (2000) *Social Care and Disability in Scotland*. York: Joseph Rowtree Foundation.

Titterton, M. (2001) 'Community Care Policy in the United Kingdom.' In J. Johnston (ed) *Community Care: History and Policy*. Milton Keynes: Open University.

Titterton, M. (2002) *Health Literacy: Working with Socially Excluded Groups, Including Prisoners and Ex-offenders*. Final Report. Ayr: Ayrshire and Arran NHS Board.

Titterton, M., Hill, M. and Smart, H. (2002), 'Mental health promotion and the early years: The evidence base. Risk, protection and resilience.' *Journal of Mental Health Promotion 1*, 1, 20–35.

Titterton, M., Smart, H., Curtice, L. and Maxwell, S. (2000) 'Supporting health promotion activity in the voluntary sector: Research findings and strategic considerations.' *Health Education Journal 59*, 364–372.

Tomison A.M. (1999) 'Ensuring the protection of children: The role of child protection services in the identification, assessment and treatment of maltreated children.' Key note presentation to child and family services workshop, New South Wales Deparment of Community Services, Sydney.

Toye, J. (1992) 'Controlling health risks at work – a challenge for training.' *Transition 92*, 8, 12–13.

Tucker, S. (2003) 'Interprofessional education: A curriculum response to work with children and young people.' *Children and Society 17*, 2, 137–148.

Ungar, S. (2001) 'Moral panic versus the risk society: The implications of the changing sites of social anxiety.' *British Journal of Sociology 52*, 2, 271–291.

United Kingdom Central Council for Nursing, Midwifery and Health Visiting (UKCC) (1992) *Code of Professional Conduct.* London: UKCC.

United Kingdom Central Council for Nursing, Midwifery and Health Visiting (UKCC) (1996) *Guidelines for Professional Practice.* London: UKCC.

Vass, A. (1996) *Social Work Competences.* London: Sage.

Wald, M.S. and Woolverton, M. (1990) 'Risk assessment: The emperor's new clothes?' *Child Welfare 69*, 6, 483–512.

Walker, S. (2003) 'Interprofessional work in child and adolescent mental health services.' *Emotional and Behavioural Difficulties 8*, 3, 189–204.

Wall, D., Eynon, R. and Bullock, A. (2000) 'An evaluation of risk management training in the West Midlands.' *Journal of Clinical Governance 8*, 4, 191–194.

Wallace, L.M., Boxall, M. and Spurgeon, P. (2004) 'Organisational change through clinical governance: The West Midlands three years on.' *Clinical Governance: An International Journal 9*, 1, 17–30.

Walton, R. (1978) 'Training for risk taking: Applications in residential care.' *Social Work Service 18*, December, 1–5.

Waterhouse, L. and Carnie, J. (1992) 'Assessing child protection risk.' *British Journal of Social Work 22*, 47–60.

Waterhouse, L., Dobash, R. and Carnie, J. (1994) *Child Sexual Abusers.* Edinburgh: Scottish Office Central Research Unit.

Waterson, J. (1999) 'Redefining community care social work: Needs or risks led?' *Health and Social Care in the Community 7*, 4, 276–279.

Webb, D. and Wright, D. (2000) 'Postmodernism and health promotion: Implications on the debate on effectiveness.' In J. Watson and S. Platt (eds) *Researching Health Promotion.* London: Routledge.

Welsh Assembly (2004) *Children and Young People: Rights to Action.* Cardiff: Welsh Assembly.

Wilkinson, R.G. (1996) *Unhealthy Societies: The Afflictions of Inequality.* London: Routledge.

Williams, L.M. and Finkelhor, D. (1991) 'Characteristics of incestuous fathers.' In W.L. Marshall, D.R. Laws and H.E. Barbaree (eds) *Handbook of Sexual Assault.* New York: Plenum.

World Health Organization (WHO) (2002) *The World Health Report 2002.* Copenhagen: World Health Organization.

Wynne-Harley, D. (1991) *Living Dangerously: Risk Taking, Safety and Older People.* London: Centre for Policy on Ageing.

Young, A.P. (1994) 'In the patient's best interests: Law and professional conduct.' In G. Hunt (ed) *Ethical Issues in Nursing.* London: Routledge.

Subject Index

Author Index